New Directions
Environment, Labour and the International Trade Agenda

*For Konrad,
With Thanks for many
Courtesies - and ideas!
Keith H. Christie 30/xi/95.*

New Directions: Environment, Labour and the International Trade Agenda

Edited by
KEITH H. CHRISTIE

Carleton University Press

© HER MAJESTY THE QUEEN IN RIGHT OF CANADA 1995 as represented by the Secretary of State for External Affairs.

This edition is published by Carleton University Press, Inc., 160 Paterson Hall, Carleton University, 1125 Colonel By Drive, Ottawa, ON, Canada K1S 5B6

Canadian Cataloguing in Publication Data:

Main entry under title:

New Directions : environment, labour and the international trade agenda

Issued also in French under title: Nouvelles directions.
Includes bibiliographical references.
ISBN 0-88629-266-2

1. Canada —Economic policy. 2. Environmental policy—Canada.
3. Canada—Commercial policy
I Christie, Keith H. (Keith Hutton), 1948-

HC113.N48 1995   338.971   C95-900342-8.

Carleton University Press gratefully acknowledges the support extended to its publishing program by the Canada Council and the financial assistance of the Ontario Arts Council.

The Press would also like to thank the Department of Canadian Heritage, Government of Canada, and the Government of Ontario through the Ministry of Culture, Tourism and Recreation, for their assistance, and the Canada-United States Law Journal, for consenting to include in this volume the Policy Staff Paper by Michael Hart and Sushma Gera, which was previously published in volume 18, 1992 of that Journal.

Cover art is "The Dawn of Man" (oil on canvas, 112.4 x 81.3 cm.) by Bertram Brooker (1888-1955), courtesy of Phyllis Brooker Smith, trustee of the Estate of M. A. Brooker, and of the National Gallery of Canada, Ottawa.

Printed and bound in Canada.

TABLE OF CONTENTS

	Foreword	ix
	Preface	xiii
I	Trade and the Environment: Dialogue of the Deaf or Scope for Cooperation? *Michael Hart and Sushma Gera*	1
II	Stacking the Deck: Compliance and Dispute Settlement in International Environmental Agreements *Keith H. Christie*	43
III	Pandora's Box?: Countervailing Duties and the Environment *Robert T. Stranks*	75
IV	Dangerous Liaisons: The World Trade Organization and the Environmental Agenda *Anne McCaskill*	93
V	The New Jerusalem: Globalization, Trade Liberalization and Some Implications for Canadian Labour Policy *Robert T. Stranks*	137
	Annex: List of Policy Staff Publications	185

FOREWORD

THE INTERNATIONAL TRADE AND PAYMENTS system has entered a prolonged period of transformation and adjustment. Cross-border flows of goods, services, investment and technology have never been greater and have never had such a profound impact on economic prospects and the way we govern our society. The collapse of State-run command economies has removed one major ideological impediment to further trade and investment liberalization. The old North-South divide is increasingly irrelevant, as the considerable diversity among developing countries expands, with many wagering successfully on getting their domestic economic fundamentals right and on trade liberalization. The marketplace is increasingly international, with many new players competing effectively for market share at home and abroad, and as sites for quality investments.

This increasingly internationalized and competitive world presents both opportunities and challenges for a relatively small economy such as Canada. The opportunities are stunning. The unilateral liberalization in many markets and the more secure access achieved through the implementation of the Uruguay Round and the NAFTA underpin economic growth and stimulate innovation that will ensure that this growth continues. Liberalization and deregulation are opening foreign doors to Canadian exports of goods and services to an unprecedented degree. As never before, the success of Canadians as a trading nation is central to our prosperity and job creation at home.

Yet the challenges are also great. We must adjust domestic practices and regulations with a view to rewarding innovation and initiative more clearly. We must take fuller advantage of our new access to foreign markets, becoming even more a nation of traders that we are at present. And we must remain in the forefront of international rule-making as the scope of trade policy continues to expand, affecting the way we perceive an ever broader array of domestic policy instruments.

Let there be no doubt. The agenda for the next stage of international trade negotiations is being set now. As negotiations have eliminated or considerably lessened more traditional trade and investment distorting practices, other policy instruments have come under increasing scrutiny—environmental regulations, labour practices, the link between corporate governance and antitrust policy, product and process standards, exchange rate "misalignments" and other issues. In addition, the international rule-making with regard to the "new" issues of only ten years ago (investment, trade in services) is still far from complete, while much critical work remains in "traditional" areas of continuing central interest for Canada (reform of agricultural subsidy practices and the use of antidumping and countervailing duties).

Canada must remain in the forefront of the rule-making across this broad front of issues because we have specific trading interests at stake and because we cannot afford to let others make the rules for us—or even worse, to resort to unilateral measures based on sheer market power rather than on mutually agreed guideposts.

Consequently, the development of our own approach to international trade rule-making should be a priority not only for governments, but for all Canadians. Many can and should contribute, including the provinces, the private sector, academic specialists, organized labour and non-governmental organizations.

Within the Department of Foreign Affairs and International Trade, the Policy Staff contributes to stimulating this broader debate on trade-related issues through the research and distribution of its Staff Papers. Each Paper is prepared under the responsibility of its author and does not necessarily represent the views of the Government. But the issues raised are real and their eventual resolution internationally will have an important impact on Canadian prosperity. Consequently, and in light of the importance of encouraging wider discussion, I commend Policy Staff for editing the present volume, which brings together a collection of recent Staff Papers on the growing international debate over trade and environmental and labour standards and their enforcement.

Taken as a whole, the Papers in this volume reveal the complexity of the issues in play and suggest a number of relevant approaches to problem-solving in this new area of international rule-making. The Papers raise concerns that merit the attention of those with an interest in the evolution of Canadian trade policy.

The Honourable Roy MacLaren
Minister for International Trade

PREFACE

THE STAFF PAPERS REPRODUCED TOGETHER in this volume are based on three premises. First, good policy must rest on a sustained analytical and factual base. Second, while by no means the only source of such work, the Department of Foreign Affairs and International Trade has researchers and practitioners with the required analytical skills and, equally importantly, the front-line experience of negotiating international agreements. Third, the exposure of these Papers to a wider audience can help deepen the domestic debate on the issues raised, strengthening the consultative process and enriching the final product—which must be good policy for Canada. The present volume is the first of a series. We plan to release a second collection (on trade remedy and competition policy issues) by the end of the year.

Written in 1992, the Hart and Gera paper provides a general introduction to the linkages between trade and environmental policies. The authors explore the integration of environmental concerns into trade policy and vice versa, and address how two quite different groups of specialists have come increasingly to share a common file, the problems trade and environmental experts are likely to encounter in their joint work and the kinds of compromises they may need to make in order to find an appropriate balance. In this regard, the authors suggest two fundamental themes. Environment-oriented trade rules should proceed on the basis of the concept of sustainable economic development (i.e., they should be both ecologically and economically sound), and new rules should not undermine the basic principles of the open trading system (i.e., they should build on and clarify existing trading rules, not overthrow them).

Christie's 1993 paper explores in greater detail the critical interface between international environmental agreements (IEAs) and their trade counterparts. He suggests that there is increasing pressure to incorporate trade sanctions into more IEAs as a primary means of making environmental commitments operational and to provide disciplines on signatories and non-signatories alike. Nonetheless, Christie agrees that the use of trade measures to achieve environmental ends must be carefully weighed in the balance of overall Canadian interests. In this regard, he focuses much of his analysis on the inadequacies of several key IEAs as presently crafted. Their combination of trade sanctions, loosely drafted environmental obligations and, in particular, the lack of effective dispute settlement mechanisms creates a framework in which the economic power of the few could prevail over a rules-based system that applies equally to all. The author accepts that trade measures may be required in certain circumstances and that ideally a dispute involving a trade measure taken for environmental reasons against another member of an IEA should normally be adjudicated under the provisions of that IEA and not under a trade agreement. But to achieve this result, he proposes a number of criteria that an IEA should meet before Canada agrees that a given IEA override our rights and obligations enshrined in international trade agreements.

In his 1994 paper, Rob Stranks addresses whether countries should agree to mobilize one particular trade mechanism, countervailing duties, to respond to environmental concerns, particularly the issue of natural resource pricing practices. He recognizes that fuller cost internalization for a particular resource (e.g., water, forests) will invariably lead to different pricing results in different countries, given varying local eco-systems including resource sustainability. Nonetheless, evidence is presented indicating that resource pricing often reflects only weakly the importance of cost internalization and that this failure makes for bad environmental policy and can have a subsidy-like impact on competitiveness. Moreover, multilateral rules for the circumscribed use of countervail to address such "subsidies," with some multilaterally agreed threshold of environmental effects, could decrease the domestic political pressure in certain countries (including the U.S. and the European Union) to take unilateral measures. This said, Stranks highlights the complexities of the issues involved and the danger that trade protectionists could capture the resource pricing debate. He raises a number of serious questions about whether multilateral agreement could be easily reached on operationalizing countervailing duty rules to address environmental concerns. He also underlines that a high degree of uncertainty exists about whether such duties would ever be effective in achieving their professed environmental objectives.

Anne McCaskill's paper (which also appeared in 1994) argues strongly that current international trade rules already provide broad scope to employ a wide range of trade measures in support of domestic environmental programmes and standards. GATT/WTO rules, however, do not and should not provide for discriminatory, unilateral measures applied extraterritorially. This said, McCaskill concurs that improvements could be made to provide clearer and more predictable access to GATT/WTO exceptions for IEAs that reflect broad international consensus on an environmental programme that includes otherwise GATT-inconsistent trade restrictions. Her paper addresses this issue in detail and suggests options for change. Equally, greater scrutiny of purportedly environmental measures that can have a severely negative impact on trade is necessary. Nonetheless, she is sceptical, on balance, about GATT/WTO "entanglement" in environmental affairs, believing that the international trading system cannot and should not be used to arbitrate environmental policy decisions.

Rob Stranks also contributes a 1994 paper in this volume on the link between trade and labour policies. He suggests that concepts such as "social dumping" and "social countervail" should be approached very cautiously. He underlines, however, that the risk of unilateral trade measures taken by the major economic powers remains real unless the international community develops a workable multilateral understanding on trade-labour linkages. Consequently, Canada should support further work internationally on certain key labour rights and standards and their link to trade. Drawing on the North American Agreement on Labour Cooperation, Stranks focusses on the enforcement of each country's own domestic law and on the development of international consensus on a minimum set of standards in the areas of health and safety regulations and the use of child and forced labour. Sanctions to back up such international rule-making, if needed at all, should draw on a menu of measures of which trade sanctions could be only one instrument. Given the need for more empirical work on these issues, Stranks proposes an accelerated fact-finding effort in the OECD and the International Labour Organization; as well as the establishment of a joint federal-provincial task force domestically, given the provinces' preponderant constitutional authority in labour matters.

Comments on the papers in this volume and our other work are welcome. The current list of Policy Staff Papers and Commentaries on economic and trade issues is reprinted at the end of this collection in the Annex. Readers can direct correspondence by mail to 125 Sussex Drive, Ottawa, Ontario K1A 0G2, or by fax to (613) 944-0375.

Keith H. Christie, Director
Economic and Trade Policy Division (CPE)
Policy Staff

I

MICHAEL HART & SUSHMA GERA

Trade and the Environment: Dialogue of the Deaf or Scope for Cooperation?

The task of statesmanship is ... to attempt to guide the nations, with all their differences in interest, power and fortune, towards a new system more capable of meeting the 'inner limits' of basic human needs for all the world's people and of doing so without violating the 'outer limits' of the planet's resources and environment. *The Cocoyoc Declaration*[1]

INTRODUCTION

IS IT POSSIBLE FOR A TRADE NEGOTIATOR and an environmental regulator to work together on the same file? This may strike some as a flippant question. It is not meant to be. Indeed, over the past few years, it has become a pressing question that deserves serious consideration.

In suggesting that environmental regulators must learn to share their file with trade negotiators, our purpose is not to be presumptuous but practical and realistic. It is through the medium of trade that national economies relate to each other and it is the framework of rules negotiated by trade specialists that govern the nature of that relationship. Because of the potential impact of environmental regulation on international competitiveness as well as the desire of environmental regulators to influence behaviour beyond national borders through trade measures, there is now a pressing need for environmental regulators to learn from trade negotiators and vice versa.

For trade negotiators, working with other subject specialists is nothing new. Fifty years ago, trade negotiations dealt largely with tariffs and quotas, i.e., government policy measures applied at the border. Trade negotiators, therefore, were usually drawn from among those people who had some experience in dealing with these matters. But as the boundaries of trade negotiations have expanded, trade negotiators have of necessity learned to deal with a much wider range of issues. Doing so required that they learn to "share" their file. Over the years, they have learned to work with industrial policy specialists, government procurement experts, competition lawyers, service industry regulators, product health and safety inspectors and more. Each of these fields has its own assumptions, goals and sensitivities. As a result, relations have not always been easy between trade negotiators and other issue specialists, but both sides have adjusted, made the necessary compromises and managed to serve the national interest as defined by the government of the day.

Trade negotiations have now expanded to touch upon the domain of environmental regulators or, put the other way, political pressure to address environmental issues is now affecting issues that may best be addressed through trade negotiations. As a result, it is now necessary for trade negotiators and environmental regulators to learn to share this file and work out common objectives.[2]

The integration of environmental concerns into trade policy and vice versa raises a variety of complex conceptual and practical concerns. The analysis of these issues is still at an early stage of development and much work remains to be done to enlarge our understanding of what is involved. Some early conclusions about the direction that work should take, however, can already be reached. In this paper we propose to explore why these two disparate groups of specialists have come to share a file by looking at developments in the international economy and in thinking about the environment, the problems trade and environmental specialists are likely to encounter and the kinds of compromises they may need to make, with particular reference to the North American Free Trade Agreement (NAFTA) negotiations as of 1992.

COMPETING IDEOLOGIES

THE TRADE/ENVIRONMENT INTERFACE contains potential for conflict that may run somewhat deeper than, for example, that between trade and competition policies or between trade and industrial policies. The popular conception is that trade and environment specialists bring not only different perspectives to the issues, but in many ways operate from within seemingly incompatible ideologies.

To a trade specialist, trade policy serves the general objective of raising economic welfare. Each facet of the trade file - trade negotiations, dispute settlement, trade relations and trade promotion—is based on the premise that that activity will help bake a bigger pie from which everyone will eventually benefit. Reducing government-imposed barriers to the free flow of goods and services is one of the time-tested ways of achieving greater prosperity through trade. While the path to freer trade may require detours such as quotas, voluntary restraint agreements and countervailing duties, the goal remains trade as unfettered as possible by government-imposed barriers. Environmental regulators, on the other hand, assume that the pie may already be too big and that activities which promote economic growth are dangerous to the long-term ecological health of the planet. Their task is to find policies and programs that will decrease pressure on a fragile biosphere and reverse such damage as has already been done, even if that goal may at times require compromises. If such policies and programs result in barriers to trade, it is a price worth paying. Antoine St. Pierre summarizes the potential for conflict between these competing values as follows:

... free-trade advocates contend that many environmental regulations are thinly disguised non-tariff barriers to trade. At the opposite end of the ideological spectrum, environmentalists lobby for environmental measures regardless of cost to industries and consumers. They also distrust the harmonization of policies brought about by trade agreements because it tends to reduce environmental standards to a lowest common denominator and to limit the range of actions available to governments in implementing environmental preservation policies.[3]

From the start, therefore, there seems to exist a basic suspicion between the two groups of specialists which might hinder their capacity to compromise and find common ground. Such suspicion is, of course, not unique. Competition regulators, for example, find international rules about dumping irrational and at odds with their efforts to promote competition. Industrial policy specialists, interested in promoting higher levels of private sector research and development, are uncomfortable with international rules aimed at curbing the ability of governments to provide various incentives. Banking regulators worry that an open trade regime will compromise their ability to maintain fiduciary standards.

Public discussion of the apparent conflict between environmental goals and trade goals provides an excellent example of the extent to which such discussion is often misinformed and even wrong. False assertions and questionable conclusions are often reflected and magnified by the popular media, more because they are sensational than because they are right. Sober and careful analysis is unlikely to gain similar widespread attention because it is often the painstaking work of experts and not readily accessible to generalists.

As a result, there has developed a high degree of public conflict and controversy around the trade/environment interface, largely due to inadequate discussions between those who passionately espouse environmental causes and those interested in promoting trade and related economic issues. Debate about the North American Free Trade Agreement illustrates the extent to which the issues involved have become misunderstood and thus easy prey for those interested in sterile confrontation and protectionist solutions. The level of conflict apparent during that debate suggests the need both for more research and for more informed public discussion.

Decisions about what to negotiate internationally and with whom involve choices from among competing objectives. What will prove an acceptable balance in one jurisdiction, however, may prove unacceptable in another due to differing national values, endowments and priorities. Thus compromises are required not only within societies, but also between societies. The perceived conflict between various public policy objectives, however, is rarely as stark as special interests would like the public to believe. Nevertheless, good public policy requires that issue specialists find common ground and determine the extent to which presumed conflicts are soundly based or proceed from prejudices and popular fallacies.

Such common ground is unlikely to be found by extremists in the trade policy and environmental camps.[4] Little purpose will be served by insisting that the patterns and volumes of trade and production must be determined solely by the dictates of the market. Trade is not just a matter of economics; it is also a matter of politics. Trade takes place within a framework of domestic and international rules set by governments responding to a range of competing interests and values, one of which is protection of the environment. It is, therefore, unrealistic to insist that environmental objectives should not be allowed to compromise trade and economic objectives. The reverse is equally valid: it is not reasonable to insist that environmental objectives take precedence over all other societal goals. Again, public policy involves making choices. In effect, however, there is little need to make choices between environmental and economic goals. Public controversy notwithstanding, it is our view that it is possible in most cases to satisfy both sets of these seemingly incompatible objectives or to find instruments that satisfy one goal while inflicting minimum damage on the other.

Much public discussion seems to be based on a series of questionable assumptions, including that:

- economic growth and environmental degradation are closely linked;
- open markets lead to economic growth and may thus exacerbate environmental degradation;
- open markets lead to pressures to liberalize (i.e., harmonize at a lower level) existing or future regulations aimed at protecting the biosphere;
- trade liberalization between industrialized and poorer countries will encourage the development of pollution havens in the latter countries as companies exploit laxer environmental regulations; and
- more stringent environmental regulation in industrialized countries will reduce the competitiveness of established industries and increase the economic welfare costs of trade liberalization.

Few of these assumptions survive serious analysis. Careful research by economic and environmental specialists alike[5] has demonstrated that:

- economic prosperity is one of the most important determinants leading to a cleaner and more sustainable environment;
- promoting economic development in third-world countries through trade and investment is one of the most efficient ways to raise environmental conditions on a global basis;
- trade-restricting measures are often the least efficient way of ensuring that prices reflect environmental costs and thus rarely achieve environmental goals and may even retard them;
- achieving environmental goals by means of trade measures lends itself too easily to protectionist abuse; and
- there is no fundamental conflict between environmental objectives and the goals and provisions of the GATT-based trade relations system, although there is room for clarification to remove any ambiguities and to strengthen the basis upon which the trade and environmental files can be made more overtly complementary.

Finding an acceptable basis upon which environmental and trade policy specialists can cooperate would thus seem to involve a number of basic concepts: it must proceed from an agreed notion of sustainable development and it must include agreed definitions of the role and limits of trade policy and environmental protection in nurturing sustainable development. We examine each of these elements in turn.

Economic Growth and the Environment

Until the beginning of the industrial revolution, the environmental impact of production and trade was relatively small and limited largely to local effects. Over the past century, however, our use of the planet's finite resources and renewables has grown exponentially and so has the impact of that use. There is broad agreement today that the result of this intensifying exploitation of our resources is increasing pressure on the environment, both locally and globally. As a result, one of the most fundamental conflicts between the trade and environmental files is the presumed conflict between economic growth and protection of the environment. Is this conflict real or imagined?

The intuitive answer many would give is that there is such a conflict. Careful analysis, however, does not bear out this conclusion. To understand why, one must begin with an appropriate concept of the goal of environmental protection, one that is consonant with public policy in a democratic society. If the goal is to halt all activities that may in any way alter the current state of the environment or return it to earlier conditions, then there may be no alternative to conflict. Such an approach to environmental regulation, however, is neither reasonable nor necessary. From time immemorial man has altered his physical environment, either consciously or unconsciously. The only constant has been continual adaptation. The operative question, therefore, is whether man has altered his environment for better or for worse. More specifically, has the human species, in changing its environment, added to or subtracted from the overall well-being of the species? When viewed from a sufficiently long and broad perspective, the answer is no. As the environment and circumstances have changed, the general well-being of most of the species has improved.

It was Thomas Malthus who first suggested some two hundred years ago that the planet's resources were finite and that if the global population continued to grow, there would eventually not be enough food to feed everyone. Since then, the basic Malthusian thesis has been refined and adapted to a wide variety of predictions about the capacity of the planet to sustain life as we know it, all of them sharing his basic pessimism. Neither Malthus nor his spiritual descendants accept the Darwinian concept of adaptation nor the potential impact of improvements in technology. Malthus' prediction of mass starvation would have happened by now if it had not been for the constant improvement in agricultural techniques as well as transportation and distribution systems, all fueled by economic growth.

A few examples should illustrate why some of the pessimism of environmental extremists is not well founded. When Malthus was writing, the combination of coal fires and the particular climatic conditions in southeastern England produced the infamous London smog. Its impact on human, animal and plant life and health was clearly unacceptable. The addition of industrial and car exhaust fumes in the twentieth century made conditions intolerable. Today, as a result of the introduction of newer technologies and stricter regulation, made possible because the inhabitants found conditions intolerable and were prepared to pay for improvements through higher prices, taxes and regulatory burdens, London smog has become an historical phenomenon. It would not have disappeared, however, if there had not been economic incentives to discover the necessary technologies and economic growth to pay for their application.

Similarly, the Cayuga River and Lake Erie were for years synonymous with environmental rape. While neither has yet been returned to an acceptable level, it is now safe to light a match when crossing the Cayuga and it will not be long before Lake Erie will once again be safe for swimming.

What these examples have in common is that the human species, having first affected the environment negatively, adapted and learned to affect it positively. The key to both changes in direction came about because markets were allowed to work. At the beginning of the process, the value of exploiting the environment negatively was less than the negative effects, leading to degradation. Once these negative effects became clear and unacceptable, appropriate steps to adapt were taken leading to an improvement.[6] As Marian Radetzki concluded at a recent World Bank symposium:

There simply is no evidence of general environmental deterioration in consequence of continued economic growth. Empirical observation suggests, if anything, the obverse relationship to be closer to the truth: that the quality of the environment improves as the density of the economy increases.[7]

In developing an acceptable approach to defining how best to achieve a cooperative trade and environment interface, therefore, the first element involves agreeing on an appropriate definition of what constitutes sustainable development. As a working hypothesis for this paper, the definition set out in the Brundtland Commission provides a good starting point:

Sustainable development is best understood as a process of change in which the use of resources, the direction of investments, the orientation of technological developments, and institutional change all enhance the potential to meet human needs both today and tomorrow.

Sustainable development does not mean that there will be no conflicts or adjustments, particularly at the micro level. The decision to protect the rare spotted owl in the U.S. Northwest, for example, has profound implications for the U.S. and Canadian lumber industries and downstream industries dependent on that lumber. The capture of sulphur from the stacks of smelters and coal-fired generating stations has changed the outlook for sulphur mining. At the same time, higher environmental standards may also lead to new opportunities. Greater environmental awareness has already proven a spur to welcoming new technologies and processes. Many Canadian and U.S. companies have been among those in the forefront in developing new products and processes that respect the fragile interaction between man and nature.

Trade and Economic Prosperity

While there does not appear to be much evidence to support the proposition that economic growth leads to long-term deterioration of the environment, there is a great deal of evidence to suggest that trade leads to economic growth. Indeed, the positive relationship between trade and economic growth is one of the oldest and most established concepts in economic theory.

Canada and the United States are prosperous countries in part because of their historically strong trade performance. Success in buying and selling on world markets has made each country a major contributor to and beneficiary of the global economy. Since the Second World War, the progressive liberalization of markets has encouraged the two economies to adjust and become more integrated into the world economy. This has allowed producers in both countries to specialize in what they do best and to let consumers buy their other requirements more cheaply from abroad. As a result, incomes in both countries have grown steadily.

Most of us are prepared to accept that exports are an important contributor to our economic well-being. We are less familiar with the importance of imports in giving us the high standard of living we all take for granted. We import in order to obtain more final and intermediate products at lower prices than we would be able to produce such products for ourselves. As a result, we are able to devote the capital, technology and people which would otherwise be used to produce the goods and services we now import to do the things we do best. Imports help to keep firms competitive and provide both firms and individuals with the latest products and technologies, including those aimed at improving the environment. Our ability to buy a wide range of competitively priced foreign products with the proceeds of our exports has left us with more money to do other things—money to serve both personal and national needs, including protection of the environment.

Trade policies that promote the most efficient use of scarce resources on an international basis will stimulate economic growth on a global basis. Trade policies that restrict access to markets and encourage the uneconomic exploitation of resources will retard growth. From an environmental perspective, the most appropriate use of resources would occur if prices were able to reflect the true costs of their production to the environment. That is more likely to happen if markets are allowed to work than if they are not. The world of agricultural trade offers a good example of market failure as a result of inappropriate trade and economic policies and the resultant pressures on the environment. Production subsidies and closed borders have resulted in highly intensive land exploitation in Western Europe at a level that is not compatible with the long-term sustainability of that land. If markets were allowed to work, European agriculture would become less intensive and more sustainable in the long term and European consumers would benefit from the lower costs of imported food products.

The second element in defining an appropriate trade and environment interface, therefore, involves acceptance of the fact that maintaining an open trade regime is key to maintaining sustainable economic development. Compromises may at times be necessary between economic and other objectives, including environmental objectives, but such compromises should be addressed within the framework of existing rules and should not undermine the basic values of an open trading system.

ENVIRONMENT POLICIES FOR SUSTAINABLE DEVELOPMENT

IN THE LAST FEW DECADES, awareness of the need to protect the fragile biosphere has approached the top of the public policy agenda. The depletion of the ozone layer, global warming, waste disposal problems and the threatened extinction of plant and animal species are just a few examples of the issues that have made protecting the environment an urgent global priority. No responsible politician today would any longer deny the importance of this issue. Business leaders have become acutely aware of the need to be sensitive to environmental concerns. The issue is no longer whether, but how. A major challenge, therefore, is to find an acceptable balance between environmental and economic goals.

As we noted earlier, the aim of environmental policy is to ensure that the planet remains a viable and rewarding place for the human species. It follows that not all activity that has a negative impact on the environment is necessarily bad nor should environmental concerns always take precedence over other societal goals. For example, modern society devours a considerable amount of energy on a daily basis. Conservation may reduce but will not eliminate the appetite for vast quantities of energy. Each of the various sources poses environmental risks. Burning coal pollutes the atmosphere; hydro-electric power may require the damming of rivers and the destruction of fragile eco-systems; nuclear power may lead to devastating accidents and requires the disposal of highly hazardous wastes; and the burning of fossil fuels contributes to global warming. Newer, less hazardous forms of energy remain as yet impractical on any large scale. Living without energy is not an acceptable solution. The challenge, therefore, is to find the best combination of imperfect instruments that will least contribute to environmental problems and at the same time not undermine maintenance of an open trading system. Concludes the World Bank's Patrick Low:

... the simple idea that environmental standards are not absolutes with infinite values turns out to be very powerful. It implies greater scope for policy flexibility. It undermines some of the less reasoned populist positions on the environment, in particular on trade and the environment, and it weakens the position of protectionists that seek to conceal their demands for trade restrictions in environmental arguments.[10]

In keeping with the goal of ensuring that economic development sustains the capacity of the globe to meet current and future human needs, measures aimed at protecting the environment should be sufficient to the objectives they are meant to achieve but not more than sufficient. Determining sufficiency is a matter both of establishing a scientific basis for the measure and also of investigating least cost alternatives, i.e., costs that reflect appropriate tradeoffs between environmental and other societal goals.

The third element in developing an appropriate approach to the trade/environment interface thus involves ensuring that environmental policies meet the standard of sufficiency, i.e., that they are a necessary and legitimate response to the problem and proportional to the goals being sought. Given differences in environmental preferences, as well as financial and technological capabilities in different countries, a great deal of analysis and consultation will be required on a case-by-case basis to develop consensus as to what constitutes sufficiency. Despite differences of view as to, for example, risk assessment, suitability and appropriate bench-marks involved in environmental measures, the sufficiency standard should provide a rational basis for dialogue as well as a standard upon which to make informed public choices and resolve intergovernmental conflict.

Environmental Policy and Trade

Environmental problems are now understood to involve a wide range of issues. Efforts to address these can be divided into two broad categories: efforts to protect the physical environment, whether water, air or land; and efforts to conserve resources, whether renewable or not, including the protection of endangered or threatened plant and animal species. In each case, the specific problems addressed can be classified as either local, regional (including transboundary) or global. The nature of the problem dictates the solution and the range of interests involved. For example, whether a particular plot of land should be used as a park, as a housing development or as a factory site will in most instances engage only local interests. If that plot of land happens to be on the border between two states and the proposed factory will involve a nuclear power facility, the issue may well engage interests on both sides of the border. If the proposed land use involves a factory that will produce ozone-depleting gases, global interests are engaged.

It is the wide range of problems and solutions and the increasing realization that more than local issues and interests must be met that has made the need to address the environmental/trade interface urgent. For our purposes, we need only concern ourselves with those environmental policies and measures that either involve trade policy measures or implicate trade flows.

Generally speaking, trade and environmental policies can be understood to intersect along two axes: meeting environmental goals may require policies that must be enforced either directly or indirectly by trade measures and/or environmental measures may affect the international competitiveness of certain producers. Conflict may thus arise between environmental and trade objectives as a result of:

- the use of trade instruments to enforce compliance with national regulations, such as restrictions on the imports of products that do not meet domestic standards;
- the use of trade measures to enforce international environmental agreements, such as sanctions, against the products of non-complying countries; and
- compliance costs borne by producers in one jurisdiction but not in another.

Controversy in the application of these measures often results from national differences in assessing the need for environmental protection and the choice of instruments used as remedies. While international harmonization would eliminate some of the conflict, it is neither reasonable nor necessary to insist on international harmonization in many instances. There should be room to allow for differences in ecological conditions, comparative advantage, social preferences and political choices among national jurisdictions. Nevertheless, there may be need for the international community to cooperate in developing common basic standards to reduce conflict and provide an improved basis for resolving disputes. International agreements facilitate national decision-making by providing a framework of rules within which to address the demands of domestic special interests. Trade agreements and trade policy measures, however, may not necessarily be the best instruments for setting environmental standards, particularly where the trade dimension is at best marginal or incidental.

Trade is rarely the cause of environmental degradation, although there are circumstances where it may draw attention to an existing environmental problem. Rather, the root cause of environmental degradation lies in the failure of markets fully to reflect environmental costs, often due to inadequate or inappropriate government policies or consumer information. Consequently, the most effective solution lies in implementing measures that will allow markets to reflect these costs more accurately and thus influence the behaviour of producers and consumers away from environmentally hostile decisions.

While trade itself is rarely the cause of an environmental problem, the products traded internationally or the processes by which they are produced may embody an environmental problem. Once a government decides to address an environmental issue that may be embodied in a tradable good or service, therefore, it must first determine whether the solution lies in the product itself or in the process by which it is produced. In deciding what approach works best, a range of instruments may be used. The choice of appropriate instruments—regulations, taxes, standards, subsidies or trade restrictions—is thus not only an environmental issue but also an issue affecting industrial policy, fiscal policy or trade policy. The final decision may ultimately require a choice involving tradeoffs between competing objectives.

Trade Measures to Enforce Compliance with Domestic Standards

All countries have in place a range of measures affecting the production, distribution and sale of domestic output as well as the necessary instruments to ensure that imported products do not undermine these measures. For example, a Canadian law banning the production and sale of a particular toxic product will also include a ban on the importation of that product. Similarly, the imposition of a domestic commodity tax at the production stage will also involve a similar tax on importation. Labelling requirements must be met by both domestic and imported products. Thus there is nothing unusual in a country's insisting that its environmental laws and regulations apply equally to domestic and imported products and using trade measures to enforce such a policy.

Problems may be encountered, however, if such measures differentiate between domestic and imported products, i.e., if the burden of compliance is heavier on imported than domestic products. While international trade law will tolerate some differentiation, it must be shown that such differentiation is necessary to meet the objectives of the policy and does not amount to a disguised restriction on trade. As we shall see below, many of the problems that have been experienced in the environment/trade interface in the past few years can be traced to the failure of governments to justify the necessity for differentiating between domestic and imported products.

A second problem may arise if the measure regulates the process by which a product is produced, rather than the product itself. If the domestic and imported products are indistinguishable but the process by which they have been produced are different, the temptation to insist that imported products must meet the same process standards will be very high. Producers that do not meet the necessary process standards, and their governments, may well complain that the trade measure being used to enforce the process standard is discriminatory. In effect, extending process standards to imported products amounts to an extraterritorial extension by one state of its laws. The result is likely to be conflict, particularly if there is not broad international consensus on the objectives being pursued by means of the process standard. Recent cases such as the U.S.-EC dispute about beef hormones, the U.S.-Mexico dispute about yellowfin tuna and Canada-EC differences on clear-cut versus selective cut forestry management practices illustrate the difficulties that can be encountered when one country adopts a different process standard from another.

A third problem may be encountered if one country is determined to conserve a particular natural resource and takes steps at its border to enforce such a policy, either through import or export measures that have the effect of differentiating between domestic and foreign producers. Both Canada and the United States, for example, restrict the export of logs. Several Canadian provinces have further processing requirements for minerals extracted in that province. Such measures may serve important environmental objectives but may also serve protectionist ends.

As we shall see below, while there are problems that may be encountered in the application of border measures to enforce domestic environmental laws and regulations, the international trade regime has to date proved adequate to the task of insisting that such measures meet certain basic standards aimed at avoiding intergovernmental conflict. There remains, however, room for improvement by, for example, developing clearer definitions and procedures attuned to new circumstances.

Trade Measures to Enforce Compliance with International Agreements

The use of trade sanctions to enforce internationally agreed environmental standards has a mixed history as regards their effectiveness and conformity with trade rules. As with any international sanctions, their effectiveness is directly related to the degree of international agreement and commitment they enjoy. Sanctions applied by only a few states to influence the behaviour of many states are unlikely to be successful. Sanctions applied by many states to influence the behaviour of a few states are much more likely to succeed.

Such sanctions are not automatically at odds with international trade rules. The experience in enforcing the Convention on International Trade in Endangered Species of Wild Fauna and Flora (CITES) offers a positive example of the use of trade measures to enforce environmental objectives. Depletion in the numbers of an endangered species such as the African elephant may be directly linked to demand for and trade in ivory. In such an event, the solution lies to a large extent in eliminating or strictly controlling that trade through trade restrictions. There has not been much international conflict about either the goal or the means in such an obvious trade-linked example. The Convention is a well established instrument and the need to use trade restrictions along these lines is well provided for in international trade law.[11] Similarly, many countries have since 1906 enforced an international ban on trade in matches made with white phosphorus as a result of an international agreement that recognized the dangers in the manufacturing process involved.[12]

Conflict may arise, however, when there is insufficient international consensus on either the environmental objectives being sought or on the need for trade restrictions to ensure compliance. Trade restrictions aimed not only at enforcing compliance by signatories but also at gaining broader participation may be challenged by non-participants on grounds of discrimination. The Montreal Protocol on Substances which Deplete the Ozone Layer, for example, imposes more onerous trade restrictions on non-signatories than signatories in an effort to expand participation and prevent the relocation or expansion of production of the banned substances in non-signatories. Its trade provisions may well be challenged by non-signatories.

Even more difficult is the use of trade sanctions by one state or a few in order to influence the environmental policies of other states. Whatever the merits of the environmental objective being sought, the unilateral use of sanctions by a powerful country or by a group of countries sets a potentially dangerous precedent for the validity of international rule-making and enforcement. It undermines the important principle that trade measures should not be used to force acceptance of other countries' policies and values except under extreme circumstances and then only when sanctioned by an international body such as the UN Security Council.

The effective use of trade sanctions to enforce compliance with internationally agreed environmental standards thus requires at least three elements: wide acceptance of the standard being enforced, broad consensus on the most appropriate and effective instrument needed to gain compliance, and broad agreement that a departure from the principle of non-discrimination is necessary and will be effective. If these conditions are met, there is unlikely to be conflict with the trade rules. If necessary, the GATT's waiver provisions could be successfully invoked. It is only when these conditions are not met that there is likely to be conflict and the trading rules in such circumstances stand as an important barrier to arbitrary and discriminatory behaviour by a minority of states or a powerful state acting unilaterally.

Trade Measures to Level the Environmental Playing Field

One of the most frequently raised concerns is that environmental protection policies undermine the competitiveness of firms because of high compliance costs. Arguments have been advanced that, unless there is broad international consensus on particular goals and instruments, governments should be allowed to take steps to "level the playing field" by taking appropriate action in the field of trade, usually by means of countervailing or offsetting duties of one kind or another.

Before considering whether trade policy should be used to level playing fields, we should consider the extent to which environmental regulations undermine competitiveness. Recent analytical and empirical work suggests that the aggregate additional costs of meeting environmental requirements in the United States add less than one per cent to the cost of doing business.[13] Aggregate costs, of course, reflect wide variation and in highly competitive industries, additional costs of even one per cent can make the difference between profit and loss. But the relative cost of compliance with existing pollution requirements appears to be modest and well within the capacity of most industries to absorb. At the same time, as pointed out by Michael Porter in his study of the Canadian economy, compliance with tough pollution standards can also prove a powerful incentive to innovation and prove an important step toward improving competitiveness.[14]

Related to concern about differential compliance costs is the fear that countries will use lower standards as an investment incentive and thus become pollution havens. Again, the evidence to support such fears is not very robust. While the assimilative capacities of some countries—particularly developing countries—to absorb or tolerate higher levels, for example, of atmospheric pollution may attract some dirty industries to relocate, the cost of relocating has to be taken into account as do other factors such as labour costs, proximity to either suppliers or customers, the availability of low-cost energy supplies, fiscal policy and other factors that influence such decisions. Additionally, experience suggests that technological improvements to meet tougher environmental standards usually go hand in hand with broader technological improvements. Thus, new investments in, for example, developing countries to replace old investments in industrialized countries of traditional "dirty" industries are likely to involve the use of the latest technologies and lead to a net reduction in global pollution levels.[15]

The whole question, however, needs to be kept in perspective. Countries trade in order to exploit the comparative advantage they derive from differing factor endowments such as available resources, the quality and price of labour, the policy environment, the costs of inputs and proximity to markets. The international trading rules seek to ensure that comparative advantage can work and lead to a more efficient allocation of scarce resources on a global basis. Efforts to put in place trade barriers aimed at levelling the playing field in effect defeat the whole basis upon which trade takes place.[16]

Pressures to level the playing field, of course, are not new. In the first years of this century, U.S. economists were much preoccupied with developing arguments for and against the so-called scientific tariff. The idea was that the U.S. tariff on individual products should be set at a level high enough to offset the cost advantages enjoyed by foreign producers but no higher.[17] The devilishly clever variable levy used by the EC to protect its agricultural producers works much the same way. The result is very little trade. While the whole concept is economic nonsense, more sophisticated versions keep cropping up. Current demands that producers facing higher environmental compliance costs in one country should be allowed to seek countervailing duties to offset these costs on imported products fall into the same category.[18] Putting aside the formidable methodological difficulties of measuring comparative costs of pollution compliance in differing jurisdictions, it would involve an intolerable unilateral intrusion into the policies of one country by another. The solution lies in negotiating international rules and standards that respect both the need to promote environmental protection and the desirability of maintaining an open trading system.

POLICY CONVERGENCE AND HARMONIZATION

TO SOME, OF COURSE, THE ANSWER lies in a much greater degree of international harmonization of product and process standards at sufficiently high levels so that environmental objectives would not be compromised by agreement around the lowest common denominator. While there has been considerable positive experience over the last ten years in reaching internationally agreed basic standards, it is neither necessary nor desirable to insist on such harmonization in all cases.[19] Indeed, much of the effort in international trade negotiations has been predicated on the desire to reduce the trade-distorting effect of differing regulatory approaches rather than on harmonization per se.

There is broad international acceptance today that different countries may rationally choose different levels of, for example, environmental protection depending on such factors as unique local conditions and different policy priorities. The impact of car exhaust fumes on the environment of Mexico City is markedly different from their impact on the environment of Regina, Saskatchewan. Additionally, there are circumstances in which governments are prepared to agree on ways and means to accept each others' standards where the detail may be different but the effect is the same.

Efforts within the EC are probably the most advanced and even within this highly integrated multi-national market, there is broad acceptance that there are legitimate reasons for different standards.

Environmentalists worry that any efforts to achieve harmonization or acceptance of equivalence will lead to acceptance of the lowest common denominator. Experience to date suggests that such fears are unwarranted. International discussions have usually accepted the principle that member states to any international standard are free to impose higher standards than the international norm, sometimes adding the proviso that such higher standards should not constitute a disguised or arbitrary restriction on trade. Additionally, pressures from business interests to accept lower standards are now more than offset by the demands of environmental groups, making such business pressures no longer credible.

Harmonization of standards is a time-consuming and resource-intensive activity and is most likely to be achieved where there is a degree of consensus on the objectives to be achieved. Even then the technical requirements may be formidable, particularly where there is already considerable experience with differing standards in different jurisdictions.[20]

Little progress toward greater uniformity in environmental standards is likely to be achieved in the absence of international cooperative efforts. At the same time, resort to unilateral trade measures aimed at enforcing unique environmental standards will likely do little more than undermine healthy international competition and harm global economic prosperity. Notes Patrick Low:

Environmental diversity and differences in assimilation capacity become part of what countries seek to take advantage of by specializing through trade, rather than what they seek to eradicate through trade restrictions and fatuous harmonization that is destructive of competition.[21]

Much standards-setting activity, of course, falls outside the scope of governments and involves cooperative efforts through industry-sponsored organizations and other private sector links such as licensing arrangements. The driving force behind this activity is the recognition that markets are global and a proliferation of standards undermines competitiveness.

The desire for greater uniformity should be seen as part of the response by governments and industry toward the globalization of production and markets. On the macro-economic side, there is growing convergence, with all governments pursuing policies aimed at ensuring price stability. On the micro-economic side, there is both convergence and rivalry with governments using a range of policy measures both to protect existing investments and attract new investment. While harmonization per se is not necessarily virtuous, environmental policy rivalry—either to attract or protect investment—would seem an inappropriate and potentially destructive approach similar to the harmful use of subsidies to attract investment. From this perspective, convergence in the use of environmental policy instruments is an important international objective.

ENVIRONMENTAL POLICY AND GATT

OVER THE PAST FEW YEARS, there has developed an active international jurisprudence on the intersection of trade and environmental policy. These cases have involved:

- a Canadian challenge of a U.S. embargo on imports of Canadian tuna justified as consistent with the requirements of GATT Article XX (g) relating to the conservation of an exhaustible natural resource;[22]
- a U.S. challenge first of Canadian export controls on salmon and herring and subsequently of landing requirements, both justified on the grounds that they were required to back up resource management practices;[23]
- a Canadian challenge of U.S. controls on the imports of lobsters below a minimum size, justified on the grounds that the trade measure was part of a resource management scheme;[24]

- a challenge by the United States of a Thai ban on the importation of cigarettes;[25] and
- a Mexican challenge of U.S. restrictions on imports of yellowfin tuna, justified on the grounds that the measure was necessary to reduce the slaughter of dolphins as a result of the fishing methods used by Mexican and other non-US. fishermen.[26]

Environmental critics of the GATT-based trade rules have suggested that these and other cases indicate that the trading rules are insensitive to modern concerns about the environment and need to be overhauled in order more clearly to establish the precedence of environmental goals over trade goals. Our reading of this jurisprudence, however, is somewhat different. In our view, these cases suggest the ease with which environmental concerns can be subverted to pursue less noble objectives. The problem, therefore, may not lie in the rules but in their interpretation or abuse. Notes Steve Charnovitz:

If the "greening" of the GATT means that the Contracting Parties should respect environmental objectives in administering Article XX, then greening is a good idea. But if greening means that the Contracting Parties should subordinate economic goals to ecological imperatives, then greening is a bad idea—for the environment and for the GATT. It is a bad idea for the environment because the GATT does not have the scientific expertise to judge what ecological measures are appropriate. It is a bad idea for the GATT because environmental policy would be too divisive for GATT's current decision-making structure.[27]

While not perfect, the GATT rules, first negotiated in 1947, provide a very solid foundation upon which to develop more detailed and more modern rules. Their genius lies in the fact that they start with an enunciation of some very basic principles which can be summarized as follows. Measures taken must be:

- non-discriminatory;
- transparent; and

- appropriate to the agreed goal of developing an open, liberal international trading system.

Should any conflict arise among member states in the application of these principles, GATT provides more detailed rules spelling out more specific obligations as well as procedures for the resolution of disputes consonant with these principles.

At least seven GATT provisions can be invoked to address trade-related environmental issues. The first is that the trade measures used by member states must be non-discriminatory. Any trade measure must apply equally to all member states (the most-favoured-nation requirement of Article I) and must not discriminate between goods of national origin and imported goods except for those GATT-sanctioned measures—largely tariffs—applied at the border (the national treatment requirement of Article III). The requirements of Article III are spelled out in much greater detail as regards the use of product standards, including the requirement that such regulations may not be used as a disguised restriction on trade and must serve a legitimate domestic objective. The GATT Technical Barriers Code does not involve the establishment of standards but it encourages international harmonization. Current Uruguay Round negotiations, however, involve improvements in the Code that may include more robust provisions leading to greater harmonization.[28]

Second, GATT measures must be applied transparently (Article X). Both domestic producers and international traders must have equal and open access to those laws, regulations and procedures that affect their ability to transact business in any market. The frequently voiced complaint by environmentalists that the trade regime discourages the use of information about the environmental impact of various products misreads the GATT. The GATT places a very high premium on information, and enjoins its members from imposing differential regulations that discriminate between domestic and imported products.

Third, GATT contracting parties (CPs) may not use quantitative restrictions (QRs) except in clearly delineated circumstances (Article XI). When quantitative restrictions are used, they must not discriminate among foreign suppliers (Article XIII). The strong bias against QRs reflects GATT philosophy that such measures are likely to be more restrictive, less transparent and more discriminatory than measures that have a direct price effect, such as tariffs. This GATT bias makes sense in an environmental context. For example, GATT allows a country to impose a tax on imported products to reflect its desire to let the final price more closely reflect environmental costs, so long as that tax is also applied to domestically produced goods. GATT does not want CPs to use QRs to achieve such objectives.

Fourth, CPs may use subsidies to achieve various domestic objectives, including environmental goals, but may not use export subsidies except for primary products (Article XVI). Subsidies must be notified but can be limited to domestic producers and products (Article III). Products that benefit from subsidies may be countervailed—a special tariff to offset the price effect of the subsidy—if imports of the subsidized product can be shown to cause material injury to domestic producers (Article VI). The rules relating to subsidies are amplified in the much more detailed subsidies code negotiated during the Tokyo Round negotiations. A new, much improved code may emerge from the current Uruguay Round multilateral trade negotiations.[29]

Fifth, should there be conflict between any GATT Article and the desire of any contracting party to protect the environment (to protect animal, plant or human life or health; to conserve exhaustible resources; or to take action to ensure compliance with a domestic regulatory requirement not otherwise inconsistent with the General Agreement), Article XX allows member states to implement the environmental protection measure so long as the measure does not constitute a disguised restriction to trade and does not unjustifiably or arbitrarily discriminate among member states.

Sixth, in the event that none of the provisions outlined above is sufficient to justify a particular course of action, the waiver provisions (Article XXV:5) allow the Contracting Parties by two-thirds vote constituting at least half of all CPs to waive any obligation contained in the agreement. The waiver route provides GATT members with the opportunity to pass collective judgment on a particular set of circumstances and avoids the need for amendment to the text. The discriminatory aspects of the sanctions enjoined by the Montreal Protocol, for example, could be regularized by a waiver should the necessary number of countries agree.

Finally, in order to prevent abuse of these various provisions, but particularly resort to Article XX, GATT's dispute settlement provisions (Articles XXII and XXIII) provide the right to challenge the policies and practices of other CPs on the ground that they "nullify or impair" benefits that could reasonably be anticipated as a result of the provisions of the agreement.

In addition to the plain language of the text, GATT law involves the interpretations placed on these rules by various GATT decisions and panel rulings. For example, the requirements of Article XX have been interpreted to include the test that any measure justified under that Article must not only not be a disguised restriction on trade, but must also be necessary to meet the stated goal and involve the least restrictive alternative.[30]

Over the years, GATT has proven a dynamic instrument capable of adapting to a range of changing requirements and circumstances, as a result of periodic negotiations, decisions, panel rulings and acceptance of regional and other arrangements imposing more stringent requirements. The need to strengthen and modernize the GATT-based trading system may be particularly acute today as a result of the explosion in international commerce and the changing nature of international business, but the basic principles remain sound. The Uruguay Round marked the latest opportunity to modernize and improve the GATT in response to these changing circumstances.

Despite our conclusion that recent cases do not indicate a pressing need to change the rules, we see a broader utility in considering whether the existing trade rules can be adapted to accommodate environmental concerns. Efforts to use trade measures to achieve environmental goals are likely to continue to increase. Consequently, it makes sense to effect such changes as can be made in order to ensure that environmental concerns can be addressed without destroying the carefully developed but fragile consensus favouring an open global economy. Additionally, environment-driven improvements in the trade rules must be considered in the broader context of remaking the trading system to address the problems generated by today's international economy.

THE ENVIRONMENT AND TRADE NEGOTIATIONS

TRADE AGREEMENTS ARE FUNDAMENTALLY about regulating government behaviour. They set out rules about what governments can do to regulate and influence the flow of goods, services, investment, technology and labour across national frontiers. The success of earlier negotiations in reducing barriers has led to a tremendous growth in world trade and in global economic integration. That increased integration has identified new areas of friction and conflict. As a result, the focus of trade negotiations is changing from measures applied at the border—tariffs and quotas—to measures and policies used by governments to regulate and influence behaviour in the domestic market. Efforts to negotiate rules about trade and the environment, therefore, are part of a larger effort to develop international standards and consensus on a wide range of issues traditionally considered to be domestic in character, such as competition policy, social policy and labour policy. These raise very difficult issues, not the least of which is the extent to which governments are prepared to raise the level of international agreement and accept new inroads into domestic economic decision-making.

This evolving agenda represents a fundamental shift in focus and will only succeed if approached carefully and incrementally. It took years to develop the current rules about border measures. It is unrealistic to expect that the necessary intellectual capital and international consensus can be developed in a few short years to address an even more complex set of issues. The major challenge today, therefore, is not *whether* we should negotiate about some of these difficult issues, but *how*. A fundamental consideration in determining how to begin to address these issues is the requirement that governments must be careful not to undermine the basic principles that underpin the global trading system.

The GATT-based system provides a framework of rules, a negotiating forum and an institutional setting aimed at promoting competition and specialization through trade. These rules may need modernization to reflect today's much more integrated and complex international economy. At the same time, governments will need to ensure that the trading system is not destroyed on the basis of questionable arguments that will ultimately undermine the capacity of governments to pursue policies that will lead to the greater prosperity that is critical to achieving a whole range of societal goals including environmental protection.

The experience in addressing subsidies and product standards shows how difficult the negotiations of the future will be. In the Tokyo Round of GATT negotiations (1973-79), governments agreed on procedural codes that aimed at reducing the ability of governments to use subsidies, countervailing duties and product standards capriciously as barriers to international trade. The Uruguay Round sought to take the next step—agreement on subsidies and standards. This proved much more difficult. Similarly, it has proven very difficult to fit rules about intellectual property protection into the framework of GATT rules because the underlying goals of intellectual property protection are very different from those found in the GATT. Rather than reducing discrimination and increasing competition, intellectual property rules seek to do the opposite.

There is, of course, international experience in negotiating rules about the environment or labour. Generally speaking, international agreements on these issues have become largely political and hortatory without the enforcement mechanisms that are central to much more contractual trade agreements.

Thus, while it is recognized that we must address these difficult issues, we must equally recognize that progress will be slow and include many false starts and noisy conflicts, at home and abroad. As a start, we need to accept that negotiations will only succeed if they proceed on the basis of the two themes explored in this paper. Environment-oriented trade rules:

- should proceed on the basis of the concept of sustainable economic development, i.e., they should be both ecologically and economically sound; and
- they should not undermine the basic principles of the open trading system, i.e., they should build on and clarify existing trading rules rather than change them.

More specifically, efforts should proceed among environmental experts to reach cooperative solutions to global environmental degradation. To the extent that such cooperation needs to be enforced by means of trade instruments, trade experts should ensure that the necessary provisions are included in the trade regime. Such provisions should build on the basic principles of GATT including non-discrimination and transparency and involve the least possible distortion of international trade.

THE ENVIRONMENT AND NAFTA

THE NORTH AMERICAN FREE TRADE NEGOTIATIONS marked the first time that environmental considerations were confronted directly in the context of a major trade negotiation. There are a number of reasons why.

- The environmental and social conditions prevailing on the Mexican side of the Mexico-U.S. border provided a ready target for those opposed to the agreement for both environmental and other reasons.
- The fact that these conditions could be related directly to a trade program—the maquiladora program based on U.S. tariff and Mexican tariff and tax concessions—sharpened

calls for addressing environmental issues in the context of the negotiations.
- Added to this was concern that lower environmental standards and/or enforcement in Mexico could act both as an incentive for pollution-intensive industries to relocate there, as well as offer "unfair" competition to industries meeting higher levels in Canada and the United States.
- There was also the related concern that lower standards and/or enforcement in Mexico could either lead to a reduction in standards throughout the free trade area or flood the Canadian and U.S. markets with lower cost and lower standard Mexican products.
- Finally, there was the general worry that trade agreements lead to more economic activity at a time when the biosphere needs less economic activity.

Some of these factors had, of course, been present in previous trade negotiations and had been taken into account. But these negotiations marked the first time that a developing country agreed to negotiate a free trade agreement with industrialized countries on a fully reciprocal basis, raising broad concerns about how the wide disparity in social, political, environmental and other conditions could be accommodated in the context of a trade agreement. These anxieties were readily exploited by those opposed to the agreement for other reasons, particularly those worried about competing with low-cost imports. The result was insistent demands that environmental concerns be addressed in the agreement. U.S. congressional support for these demands ensured that the NAFTA negotiators would have to pay close attention to this file.

From the outset, all three countries committed themselves to ensuring the highest level of cooperation in meeting environmental objectives, both in the agreement for trade-related environmental issues and in parallel discussion for broader environmental issues. In all three countries, the views and concerns of environmental activists were actively solicited to ensure that the discussions would be informed and productive.

The NAFTA negotiations thus offered a concrete opportunity to determine how the competing objectives of trade negotiators and environmental regulators could be accommodated within or alongside a trade agreement.

To set the stage, however, we must first dismiss any notion that Mexico has any interest in ignoring its environmental problems or in becoming a pollution haven. Mexico is determined to achieve as high a standard of environmental protection and clean-up as its economic circumstances will allow. The main impediment to moving faster and more thoroughly is money; a trade agreement offering higher prosperity remains a key ingredient in Mexico's long-term approach to environmental protection, a point noted by the National Wildlife Federation in the United States in its endorsement of the negotiations.[31]

As we have seen, the existing GATT-based international trade regime already provides a good basis upon which to resolve most conflicts between environmental and trade objectives. The rules, however, are not perfect and could benefit from clarification. For example, the international community has sought for more than thirty years to reach consensus on what constitutes a subsidy in order to develop more sensible rules about which kinds of government practices should be subject to the discipline of international subsidy rules.[32] Once agreement was reached on this central issue, however, it proved possible to agree that certain kinds of government assistance aimed at promoting better environmental practices should be exempted from countervailing duties. Such a provision was included in the December 1990 Brussels text which was meant to conclude the Uruguay Round of GATT but disappeared a year later in the so-called Dunkel text, issued on the authority of GATT Director-General but reflecting a further year of negotiations.[33]

The NAFTA provided a further opportunity to strengthen and clarify the existing trade rules along similar lines. As a result, negotiators from all three countries were seized with the need to meet this objective. Their efforts concentrated in three areas:

- ensuring that each country can maintain or create, as necessary, the highest environmental standards for traded goods compatible with their domestic requirements and international agreements, including all technical regulations and related approval procedures affecting human health, safety and environment;
- improving the GATT-based provisions setting out the environmental exceptions (Article XX: b and g); and
- ensuring that the dispute settlement and institutional provisions are adequate to the task of resolving conflicts that may arise in the environmental area.

It must be accepted that the negotiating goals were modest, since neither the intellectual capital nor negotiating experience was as yet sufficient to go much further. NAFTA represented, however, an important incremental step toward gaining both the intellectual capital and negotiating experience necessary for possibly more ambitious negotiations in the future.

In addition to devising better rules to resolve potential conflict between trade and environmental goals, environmental concerns affected the NAFTA negotiations in three other ways.

- Concern was expressed about Mexico's capacity to *enforce* its environmental laws and regulations and the consequent threat that Mexico could become a pollution haven and a source of unfair competition. Mexico's capacity to enforce its laws—environmental or other—will be enhanced as it becomes more prosperous. To the extent that the NAFTA should increase trade and other economic opportunities, it should increase Mexico's prosperity and thus its enforcement capacities. Reaching an acceptable level of enforcement can be further enhanced by Canada and the United States through *technical cooperation*. By means of parallel discussions on environmental issues, Canadian and U.S. environmental officials are working with Mexican officials to find the most effective ways to provide technical assistance.[34]

- There is broad consensus today that the rapid economic development of the Mexico-U.S. *border region* through the maquiladora program placed unacceptable environmental pressures on the region, particularly on its water supplies. This is largely an issue between the United States and Mexico and is being addressed bilaterally. The United States has to date committed $700 million and Mexico $500 million to phase one of an extensive cleanup program. Experts suggest that more may be required.[35]
- Both Canada and the United States have committed themselves to conducting an *environmental assessment* of the agreement. This may prove a formidable task. In the case of projects such as dams, roads and buildings, such a review is relatively straightforward to implement. When it comes to a comprehensive trade agreement involving changes to potentially several dozen statutes and even more policies and programs, the task can be complex and vast. In effect, such an audit seeks to determine the future impact of a policy instrument that sets out rules about how governments will regulate the conduct of private parties. The number of possible variations is immense.

Fascination with predicting results is, of course, not limited to environmental concerns. Economists have long tried to model the impact of trade agreements on the economy as a whole, on individual sectors and on job creation, usually with not very precise outcomes. The results of these models tend to be most credible at high levels of aggregation and become less so as they become more detailed. Environmental assessments are likely to suffer from the same basic defect. Nevertheless, NAFTA will provide an important opportunity to explore some of the methodological problems and the limits of what can usefully be done along these lines.[36]

While technically not part of the formal trade negotiations, all three issues were linked to them and would not have been pursued in the absence of the negotiations. A more formal link could be established between the first two and the trade negotiations by means of the preamble to the trade agreement as well as by ensuring that the consultation provisions of the agreement can be used to advance environmental cooperation in both trade-related and other aspects of environmental protection.

The NAFTA negotiations mark an important, although modest step in the evolution of trade and environmental policy. In the approach taken, the three governments provided important guidance for the future. They accepted the legitimacy of addressing environmental issues within the context of a trade negotiation, but they also indicated that, while some issues are integral to the negotiating agenda, such as standards-setting rules, others can best be addressed in parallel discussions, such as technical assistance to improve enforcement of domestic rules.

CONCLUSIONS

IN THE YEARS TO COME, as global economic integration deepens and awareness of environmental issues intensifies, potential conflicts between trade and environmental goals and practices are likely to proliferate, both domestically and internationally. In response, it will be important that governments develop the necessary tools and policy instruments to resolve these conflicts equitably and quickly. As this paper has suggested, there is no inherent reason why there need necessarily be conflict. Nevertheless, there is scope to improve and strengthen the international legal framework within which inter-state conflict arising out of the trade/environment interface will need to be addressed. The basic principles enshrined in the GATT provide a sound basis upon which to build. The NAFTA negotiations provided an opportunity to begin to work out some of the practical difficulties involved. The answer to the question posed at the beginning, therefore, is yes. Trade negotiators and environmentalists can work together. Indeed, they have already started working together and the results to date are encouraging.

FOOTNOTES

1. The Cocoyoc Declaration was adopted at the Cocoyoc Symposium on "Patterns of Resources Use, Environment, and Development Strategy," held in Cocoyoc, Mexico, October 1974.
2. The need for this cooperation is now widely recognized. Both GATT and the OECD have established working groups drawing on both trade and environmental specialists. See, for example, GATT, *Trade and Environment: Factual Note by the Secretariat* (L/6896 of 18 September 1991), OECD, *Environment and Trade: Major Environmental Issues,* March 1991 (ENV/EC (91) 4) and *Synthesis Report: The Environmental Effects of Trade,* January 1992 (COM/ENV/TD (92) 5).
3. Antoine St. Pierre, *Impact of Environmental Measures on International Trade,* Report 76-91-E (Ottawa, Conference Board of Canada, 1991), p. 3.
4. Notes Stewart Hudson of the National Wildlife Federation in the United States:
"Much of the debate on trade and environment has centered on demonstrating the relative merits of free trade or protectionism, or open or closed economies, in dealing with environmental problems. If these problems are discussed in the context of sustainable development, a more optimal use of collective brainpower would be spent in identifying the emerging issues of trade and environment, and raising the questions that need to be resolved in order for world trade to promote sustainable development."
See "Trade, Environment, and the Pursuit of Sustainable Development," in Patrick Low, ed., *International Trade and the Environment,* World Bank Discussion Paper 159 (Washington: World Bank, 1992), p. 59.
5. This work is very ably summarized in a series of papers presented at a World Bank Symposium edited by Patrick Low, *International Trade and the Environment,* World Bank Discussion Paper 159 (Washington: World Bank, 1992). Another good overview is provided by Peter A. G. van Bergeijk, "International Trade and the Environmental Challenge," Journal of World Trade, vol. 25, no. 6 (December 1991), pp. 105-115 which includes extensive bibliographic references.
6. Economists explain this phenomenon in terms of an inverted U curve. Conflict between north and south in the preparations for the UN Conference on the Environment and Development, for example, reflect differences of view on where countries see themselves on this U curve.

7. Marian Radetzki, "Economic Growth and Environment," in Patrick Low, ed., *International Trade and the Environment,* World Bank Discussion Paper 159 (Washington: World Bank, 1992), p. 127.
8. World Commission on the Environment and Development (Brundtland Commission), *Our Common Future* (New York: Oxford University Press, 1987), p. 46.
9. Michael Porter in *Canada at the Crossroads: The Reality of a New Competitive Environment* (Ottawa: Business Council on National Issues, 1991), pp. 92-5 points out that the more stringent regulatory requirements, including tougher environmental standards, faced by Scandinavian forest products companies, was a key ingredient in making them more innovative and more competitive than their Canadian counterparts.
10. Patrick Low and Raed Safadi, "Trade Policy and Pollution," paper presented at the Symposium on International Trade and the Environment, World Bank, Washington, November 21-22, 1991, pp. 8-9.
11. "Trade and Environment: Factual Note by the Secretariat," GATT document L/6896 of 18 September 1991 provides a good description of CITES from a trade policy perspective.
12. Steve Charnovitz, "Exploring the Environmental Exceptions in GATT Article XX," *Journal of World Trade Law,* vol. 25, no. 5 (October 1991), provides a number of historical examples of successful environment-based trade restrictions.
13. Patrick Low indicates that for the United States the weighted average cost of pollution abatement and control equipment was 0.54 per cent, with the highest ratio, for the cement industry, being just over three per cent. See "Trade Measures and Environmental Quality: Implications for Mexico's Exports," in Patrick Low, ed., *International Trade and the Environment,* World Bank Discussion Paper 159 (Washington: World Bank, 1992), p. 107.
14. Michael Porter, *Canada at the Crossroads: The Reality of a New Competitive Environment* (Ottawa: Business Council on National Issues, 1991).
15. See, for example, Nancy Birdsall and David Wheeler, "Trade Policy and Industrial Pollution in Latin America: Where are the Pollution Havens?," Patrick Low and Alexander Yeats, "Do 'Dirty' Industries Migrate?," and Piritta Sorsa, "GATT and Environment: Basic Issues and Some Developing Country Concerns," in Patrick Low, ed., *International Trade and the Environment,* World Bank Discussion Paper 159 (Washington: World Bank, 1992).
16. See John Jackson, *The World Trading System: Law and Policy of International Economic Relations,* (Cambridge, Mass: MIT Press, 1991), particularly pp. 208-10.

17. See Jacob Viner, "The Tariff Question and the Economist," reprinted in International Economics (Glencoe, Illinois: The Free Press, 1951).
18. The fact that countervailing duties are assessed for a variety of other, equally dubious reasons, almost exclusively by the United States exercising its economic muscle, in no way justifies the use of this draconian measure for environmental reasons. The whole concept that trade must be "fair," a notion particularly popular among Washington lawyers, lobbyists and legislators, has no intellectual foundation. See James Bovard, *The Fair Trade Fraud* (New York: St. Martin's Press, 1991) for a devastating survey of what is wrong with the fair trade concept.
19. For example, in the World Health Organization (WHO), the Food and Agriculture Organization (FAO) and the International Standards Organization (ISO).
20. The slow progress in the technical discussions on phytosanitary regulations mandated by the Canada-United States FTA provide a valuable object lesson in this regard. Article 708 of the FTA provides for an ambitious work program aimed at reducing to the maximum extent possible barriers to trade resulting from differing health and phyto-sanitary regulations. Canada and the United States, despite enjoying highly integrated markets and very similar philosophies about health protection, have found it very difficult to accept each other's standards or to reach agreement on common or harmonized standards.
21. Patrick Low and Raed Safadi, "Trade Policy and Pollution," paper presented at the World Bank Symposium on International Trade and the Environment, Washington, November 21-22, 1991, pp. 8-9.
22. GATT, *Basic Instruments and Selected Documents* (BISD), vol. 29 (1981-82), pp. 91ff. The panel ruled that the measure had discriminated against Canada and could not be justified under Article XX (g) because there was insufficient evidence that the United States had taken steps to conserve tuna either through domestic production or consumption measures.
23. The GATT panel ruled that Canada's export prohibition "could not be deemed to be primarily aimed at the conservation of salmon and herring stocks and rendering effective the restrictions on the harvesting of these fish... [and] were not justified by Article XX (g)." GATT, BISD, vol. 35 (1987-88), pp. 98ff. The FTA panel ruled that the landing requirement was similarly inconsistent because it also was not aimed primarily at conservation. The landing requirement could be made consistent if a certain percentage was made available for export at a level that would still allow the remaining catch to be landed and counted as part of a conservation management scheme.

"In the Matter of Canada's Landing Requirement for Pacific Coast Salmon and Herring," Final Report of panel constituted under chapter 18 of the Canada-United States FTA, October 16, 1989.
24. "In the Matter of United States Minimum Size Requirement for Atlantic Coast Lobster," Final Report of panel constituted under chapter 18 of the Canada-United States FTA, May 25, 1990. The panel ruled that the United States requirement was consistent with its GATT obligations because it applied equally to both imports and domestic production.
25. GATT, BISD, vol. 37 (1989-90), pp. 200ff. The panel ruled that the import ban on cigarettes was inconsistent with Article XX (b) because other means were available to Thailand to control the quantity and quality of cigarettes consumed consistent with its health objectives without discriminating against imported products.
26. Gary Clyde Hufbauer and Jeffrey J. Schott, *North American Free Trade: Issues and Recommendations* (Washington: Institute for International Economics, 1992), p. 143. The panel report rejected the U.S. claim that its measure was consistent with its GATT requirements, ruling that it could not extend a process requirement extraterritorially to products indistinguishable from those produced by domestic producers. In effect, it ruled that GATT applies to like products, not processes.
27. Steve Charnovitz, "Exploring the Environmental Exceptions in GATT Article XX," *Journal of World Trade Law*, vol. 25, no. 5 (October, 1991), p. 55. This Article provides a detailed and convincing discussion of GATT law and environmental protection. Typical of negative environmental assessments of the GATT is Steven Shrybman, "International Trade and the Environment: An Environmental Assessment of Present GATT Negotiations," *Alternatives*, vol. 17, no. 2 (1990), pp. 20-9.
28. Editor's Note: The Uruguay Round negotiations concluded in early 1994, with ratification occurring by the end of the year in most contracting parties. Consequently, the Uruguay Round agreements (including an improved Technical Barriers Code) entered into force on January 1, 1995.
29. Editor's Note: In fact, the Uruguay Round did result in such an improved code.
30. This was the conclusion reached by the panel appointed under the terms of chapter 18 of the Canada-US FTA to adjudicate the Canada-U.S. dispute about landing requirements for salmon and herring in the West Coast fishery. "In the Matter of Canada's Landing Requirement for Pacific Coast Salmon and Herring," Final Report, October 16, 1989. While not a GATT panel, its findings interpreted GATT law as applied between Canada and the United States and thus

forms part of the interpretations and rulings that will guide the policies of member states as well as any GATT panel constituted to adjudicate any similar issue.
31. Gary Clyde Hufbauer and Jeffrey J. Schott, *North American Free Trade: Issues and Recommendations* (Washington: Institute for International Economics, 1992), p. 131. Hufbauer and Schott provide a detailed account of Mexican environmental laws and policies as well as efforts to improve the enforcement of these laws on pp. 135-43.
32. Michael Hart discusses the difficulties encountered in reaching consensus on international rules regarding subsidies in "The Canada-United States Working Group on Subsidies: Problem, Opportunity or Solution," Occasional Paper number 3, Centre for Trade Policy and Law (Ottawa, 1990).
33. See the draft subsidies code in MTN.TNC/W/35/Rev 1 of December 3, 1990, pp. 83-134.
    Editor's Note: The partial exemption of environmental subsidies from possible countervailing duty action reappeared in the final MTN subsidies agreement.
34. Editor's Note: Subsequently, the continuing concern about Mexico's ability to enforce its environmental standards led to the negotiation in 1993 of the North American Agreement on Environmental Cooperation - the so-called environmental "side agreement."
35. Gary Clyde Hufbauer and Jeffrey J. Schott, *North American Free Trade: Issues and Recommendations* (Washington: Institute for International Economics, 1992), pp. 144-6 offer a range of sensible suggestions on further steps than can be taken to clean up the border region.
36. Editor's Note: Canada's environmental assessment of the NAFTA was completed and released in the autumn of 1992.

II

Keith H. Christie

Stacking the Deck: Compliance and Dispute Settlement in International Environmental Agreements

Let me tell you, if you think these issues are gonna go away, you've got another think comin'. *U.S. Trade Representative Mickey Kantor (August 1993)*

INTRODUCTION[1]

THE "GREENING" OF THE PUBLIC POLICY DEBATE over the last ten years or so has been remarkable. The appeal of environmentalism cannot be underestimated. It reflects concerns, often well-founded, close to the everyday life of voters. It is easily packaged for emotional public debate, and yet addresses significant, very real-world problems at the heart of economic and social development. The combination of political sex appeal and substantive merit is powerful.

As public concern about environmental conditions increases, so has the response of governments. While much of the focus remains domestic (and properly so), governments are also faced with growing demands for solutions related to global commons issues (e.g., climate change, ozone layer depletion), transboundary pollution impacts (e.g., North American air quality), and the spectre of companies flocking to "pollution havens" in other countries (the on-going NAFTA debate about Mexican environmental standards is illustrative).

In order to foreclose unilateral action on the part of one or a very limited number of governments and in recognition that effective, long-term responses depend on mutually reinforcing cooperation, countries have increasingly turned to the negotiation of international environmental agreements (IEAs) as the bedrock upon which they can and should make progress. A fairly comprehensive 1991 list of treaties and other agreements in the field of the environment reveals that 24 were negotiated from as early as 1921 through the 1950s; another 26 in the 1960s; 46 more in the 1970s; and 56 in the 1980s.[2] Moreover, the importance of these agreements appears to have increased *qualitatively* as well. The key instruments related to ozone depletion and the transboundary movement of hazardous wastes date from the most recent period. The Canada-U.S. Air Quality Agreement, the 1992 Earth Summit conventions on Climate Change and Biodiversity, the 1993 North American Agreement on Environmental Cooperation, and the possibility of a Global Forests Convention and a regime covering the effective management of straddling fish stocks: all this recent and future activity attests to the growing range and complexity of the issues in play and of the rules of the game under development.

More is now expected of such IEAs. Negotiators carry a heavier burden and must be aware of and endeavour to reconcile a broader range of interests. For example, there are powerful voices that emphasize the need to discipline states that are not signatories of certain IEAs, especially those dealing with issues affecting the global commons. Indeed, a strong case can be made about the importance of disciplining "rogue" States, whose activity might otherwise undermine the efforts of the international community. In this regard, the denial of certain benefits (e.g., technical assistance) might be sufficient. In other instances, trade measures have been suggested. Only approximately 20 existing IEAs include trade provisions, about half related directly to the protection of flora and fauna.[3] Of these, only three provide for differences in the trade measures affecting Parties and non-Parties (more restrictive measures against the latter are found in the Montreal Protocol on Ozone Depleting Substances and the Basel Convention on the Transboundary Movement of Hazardous Wastes, as well as pursuant to several Resolutions adopted by members of the Endangered Species Convention—CITES). Nonetheless, there is increasing pressure to incorporate trade measures into more IEAs as a primary means of making the environmental commitments operational and to provide discipline on signatories *and* non-signatories alike.

Yet, there is presently enough experience with this particular trade and environment linkage to permit us to stand back for a moment and take stock. It would be useful to reflect on the key issues in play. First, it is worthwhile to underline again that, for a trading nation such as Canada that depends much more on our major markets than they depend on ours, the use of trade measures to achieve other ends must be carefully weighed in the balance of overall Canadian interests.

Second, a country may not associate itself with a particular IEA for any number of reasons: there may be an intent to "free-ride" off the commitment of others for commercial or economic advantage; there may be a sincere disagreement as to the proposed allocation of responsibilities for fixing a specific problem; the issue in play might legitimately be a lower priority for some countries than for others; and/or a non-signatory may find the scientific evidence in play to be unconvincing.[4] Although this range of reasons need not freeze the international community (or a significant proportion thereof) into obligatory passivity, it should, at least, make us cautious about rushing off too quickly to discipline non-signatories on issues for which the driving force may be as much political as environmental/technical.

Third, where discipline is deemed necessary against both signatories and non-signatories, there is no clear rationale for choosing trade as the instrument of choice, although clearly it is the weapon first thought of in most instances (all too often, in particular, by those who wield the biggest sticks).

Fourth, balance and equity suggest that sanctions against non-Parties are most convincingly justified when the IEA in question has attracted the support of a broad range of countries, where it contains obligations that are precise and no less onerous on Parties than the policy discipline aimed at non-Parties, *and* when signatories accept to discipline their *own* actions in practice with regard to the obligations of an agreement. In this regard, the development of effective compliance provisions, including a dispute settlement mechanism, are critical.

Fifth, governments need to reconcile environmental objectives (as incorporated in a specific IEA) with trade obligations and objectives (as enshrined in the General Agreement on Tariffs and Trade in the first instance). How do we achieve a reasonable and responsible balance? Exemptions to GATT disciplines (or those contained in other comprehensive trade agreements) should not be created lightly. Neither should a rogue non-signatory nor a delinquent Party to a broadly based IEA be able to hide easily behind trade agreement cover.

In this Paper, I explore several of these issues further. The primary focus is on the nature of the discipline placed on Parties to IEAs. The inter-action with non-Parties is introduced largely as an illustrative counterpoint to help us to explore this central theme. The next section contains a brief summary of the nature and extent of the obligations contained in several international environmental agreements that include trade measures, pointing out ambiguities in or exceptions to these obligations. This discussion is followed by an analysis of the dispute settlement mechanisms found in these same IEAs. The next section comprises a review of the sanctions issue, including lessons from the recently concluded North American Agreement on Environmental Cooperation. Finally, the conclusion identifies a number of guideposts derived from this inquiry.

THE INSTRUMENTS AND THE OBLIGATIONS

The Montreal Protocol

The first concrete example relates to an important global commons issues: the production and consumption of chemical substances that cause the deterioration of the ozone layer, thereby threatening human health and the environment as a result of increasing levels of ultra-violet solar radiation that reaches the Earth's surface. In this regard, scientific research has focussed on a range of substances, including chlorofluorocarbons (CFCs), halons, hydrochlorofluorocarbons and other chemicals.

The international community moved slowly at first to meet the challenge, but with an increasing sense of urgency and some creativity. The first significant multilateral legal instrument established was the Vienna Convention for the Protection of the Ozone Layer, concluded in 1985 with entry into force in September 1988. As of mid 1993, 125 countries had ratified the Vienna Convention.[5] The emphasis of the Convention is on encouraging research and exchanging scientific, socio-economic, commercial and legal information relevant to overarching obligations to protect human health and the environment against adverse effects resulting from the depletion of the ozone layer. Indeed, during their first meeting (or Conference) held in 1989, member countries identified the Convention as the "most appropriate instrument for harmonizing the policies and strategies on research" related to the ozone layer.[6]

The Convention has two other important features. First, it serves as an umbrella agreement pursuant to which governments may adopt more detailed protocols to implement measures aimed at controlling or reducing activities that have affected or are likely to affect the ozone layer negatively. Second, the Convention contains dispute settlement provisions that apply to the enforcement of such protocols, as well as of the Convention proper.

The first, and to date the only, protocol established pursuant to the Convention is the well-known Montreal Protocol on Substances that Deplete the Ozone Layer, concluded in 1987, with entry into force in January 1989. As of mid 1993, 122 countries had ratified the basic Protocol drafted in the Montreal meeting. The Protocol as drafted in 1987 established a schedule for the phase-out of a limited list of CFCs and halon gases. Since that time, there have been five meetings of member countries, during two of which in particular (London in 1990 and Copenhagen in 1992) decisions were taken which significantly expanded the list of "controlled substances" scheduled for phase-out, accelerated the pace of substance elimination (especially as a result of the Copenhagen meeting), provided further precision with respect to several key terms and concepts, established a number of institutions and rules of procedure governing the operation of the Protocol, fleshed out what to do in cases of non-compliance with the Protocol's obligations, and established a Multilateral Fund aimed at assisting developing countries in meeting the phase-out and other related obligations of the Protocol.[7]

Accelerations (called "adjustments") of the phase-out schedules for substances previously listed in the Protocol took effect almost immediately following approval in the London and Copenhagen Meetings of Parties, for those countries that had already accepted the former version of the schedules. On the other hand, amendments of the schedules in those same two Meetings which *expanded* the list of substances have required formal ratification. The relevant London Amendment (which included several other fully halogenated CFCs, carbon tetrachloride and methyl chloroform) achieved minimum adherences and entered into force in August 1992 (65 countries had ratified by mid 1993). The relevant Copenhagen Amendment (which included hydrochlorofluro-carbons, hydrobromofluorocarbons and methyl bromide) was scheduled to enter into force in January 1994 if there were at least twenty states which had ratified this latest amendment by that time.

One of the more controversial features of the Montreal Protocol is the different treatment meted out to non-Parties. Put simply, the Protocol as drafted finds non-Parties guilty by the mere fact of being a non-Party (the purest form of expedited dispute settlement!) and *obliges* Parties to ban two-way trade with non-Parties in many of the controlled substances.[8] Moreover, provision is made to ban imports of products *containing* certain controlled substances. The first stage in this process was reached in June 1991 with the adoption of a list of products containing certain CFCs and halon gases, the importation of which from non-Parties could be prohibited. The products include air conditioning units, refrigerators and other related home appliances, most aerosol products and some additional goods.[9] The Protocol anticipates a further broadening of this kind of prohibition by 1996 and 1998. Parties may also determine[10] the feasibility of banning or restricting imports from non-Parties of goods *produced with, but not containing* certain controlled substances identified in the Protocol, although the recent Fifth Meeting of Parties in Bangkok decided that it is not feasible to impose a ban or restriction on the importation of such goods produced with certain CFCs and halons under the Protocol "at this time". Finally, Parties are to discourage the export to a non-Party of technology for producing and for utilizing most of the controlled substances.

Member countries have softened somewhat the application of these prohibitions. Pursuant to Article 4.8, Parties in the 1992 Meeting agreed to waive the above restrictions for

Colombia, as that country had submitted data indicating that it was in full compliance with the appropriate limits on production and consumption of controlled substances. Furthermore, in another 1992 decision the Parties demonstrated further flexibility by determining that non-Parties which had, by March 1993, provided notification, with supporting data, of compliance with the Protocol's obligations were deemed to be in compliance with the Protocol until the next full Meeting of Parties.[11] Regardless of this flexibility, the provisions against non-Parties are, as written, stern. The importance of preventing free-riders from undermining disciplines that are central to protecting the global commons justifies such a discriminatory use of trade measures in the view of many observers.

Yet, what have *Parties* agreed to do and how is compliance ensured? As suggested above, the key undertakings are to phase-out the consumption and production of ozone-depleting substances: halon gases by 1994; CFCs, carbon tetrachloride, methyl chloroform and hydrobromofluorocarbons by 1996; and hydrochlorofluorocarbons by 2030. The commitments, however, are subject to a number of potentially important caveats. Among the more interesting, we find that:

- Parties can continue to consume recycled or used controlled substances, as these amounts are excluded from consumption and production targets, as are amounts used entirely as feedstock in the manufacture of other chemicals.[12]
- The phase-out is not absolute for Parties which are developing countries meeting certain criteria—for example, LDCs may continue to produce halon gases up to 15 per cent of 1986 levels indefinitely in order to "satisfy ... basic domestic needs".[13]
- Moreover, two-thirds of the Parties present and voting in an annual Meeting can permit "the level of production or consumption that is necessary to satisfy uses agreed by them to be essential".[14] This provision was added in 1990 in London for halon gases, but was extended to many other controlled substances two years later in the face of growing

industry concerns about the viability of identifying suitable substitute chemicals. A work programme is underway to identify specific essential uses. While this mechanism has not been used yet, it clearly allows Parties a procedure for justifying non-compliance with the original intent of the Protocol, while continuing to ban trade with non-Parties.[15]
- LDCs which are Parties (all except Bahrain, Malta, Singapore and the United Arab Emirates) are entitled to delay for ten years compliance with the phase-out schedule.[16]
- These same LDCs can claim an exemption from implementing any or all phase-out obligations if technical assistance financing (including through the Multilateral Fund established under the Protocol) *and* actual technology transfer "under fair and most favourable conditions" are felt by an LDC to be "inadequate". This unilateral decision will stand in practice unless overturned in a Meeting of the Parties by a triple majority mechanism requiring a two-thirds vote overall, representing at least a majority of eligible LDCs and of other Parties. Not an easy threshold to overcome.[17]

The Basel Convention

Over the last 30 years, billions of tonnes of hazardous wastes have been dumped or otherwise disposed of in landfills. Industrialized countries account for 95 per cent of the global production of such wastes. The transboundary movement of this material is estimated in the millions of tonnes, with many developing countries and non-governmental groups urging a ban on such exports to LDCs.[18]

In light of the risk of damage to human health and the environment posed by hazardous and certain other wastes, 116 countries negotiated the 1989 Basel Convention to regulate the transboundary movement and subsequent disposal of such material. The Convention entered into force in 1992, with the first meeting of the governing body (the Conference of the Parties) occurring in December of that year. At that time, only 35 countries had actually ratified the Convention, including Canada, France, the Nordics and several developing countries such as Mexico, but excluding most of the major generators of hazardous wastes: the U.S., Germany, Italy, Japan, Russia and the U.K.[19]

Parties to the Convention undertake obligations, many of which, regrettably, are ambiguous and open to varying interpretations and, potentially, *de facto* rule-making.

The Convention lists several categories of hazardous wastes (Annexes I and III), but also allows any Party to expand that list unilaterally in keeping with local law.[20] This is fine, it can be argued, in terms of ensuring that each country can define its own level of protection. But it also has the potential indirect result of unilaterally limiting exports to another country that may be prepared to accept such wastes for disposal, recovery or recycling.

For their part, "other" wastes are listed separately (Annex II) and currently comprise two categories: wastes collected from households, and residues arising from their incineration. It is not clear whether household wastes could include newspapers, cans and bottles destined for increasingly important commercial recycling through a parallel collection system (e.g., residential "blue boxes"). Many officials familiar with the still incipient Basel practice state that Basel is not intended to cover this material. Support for this view can be found in a 1992 OECD Decision on wastes destined for recovery, which makes an apparently sharp distinction between household waste (on the amber list subject to special transboundary movement controls) and a range of non-hazardous wastes on a "green" list (including newspapers and other paper products) subject only to normal commercial transaction controls if any.[21]

Yet, the scope of this obligation is less clear that it appears at first, providing room for "creative" interpretations and consequent disputes. The OECD Council Decision was concluded pursuant to Article 11 of Basel and thus is relevant for understanding the issue of "other" wastes in that context.[22] The Decision states that even if wastes are "green-listed," an OECD country can nonetheless control trade in such materials "as if these wastes had been assigned" to the more restrictive lists, if a Member country believes such action to be necessary to protect human health *and the environment*.[23] For example, a Member country could claim that the importance of domestically recycling used newspapers and other paper products to protect the environment (*whose* environment is not specified) is sufficient to merit the amber regime, which includes the right of the exporting country to prohibit or otherwise restrict the export of the waste in question.[24]

Moreover, Parties to Basel have provisionally approved technical guidelines on wastes collected from households which clearly cover reusable material such as bottles and cans, and recyclable material such as paper, and refer to segregating recoverable from hazardous wastes, including through "separate"/"sophisticated" collection and recovery programmes.[25] This could well be interpreted to include the increasingly important newspaper recycling business (to the degree it depends on a distinct household collection programme) within the scope of Basel's controls.

There are other ambiguities. Each Party must take "appropriate" measures to ensure the availability of "adequate" disposal facilities.[26] An exporting State must not allow the export of hazardous or other wastes "if it has reason to believe that the wastes in question will not be managed in an environmentally sound manner" in the importing State (Article 4(e)).[27] And how is a Party to interpret the critical concept of "environmentally sound manner"? The Convention provides no clear guidance, opening the door to differing interpretations (including those pursued by special interest groups) and disputes.[28] Criteria approved provisionally by the Parties in December 1992 are little better. They are impregnated with disputable concepts such as "adequate" standards, "appropriate" monitoring of disposal sites, "appropriate" action when "unacceptable" emissions result from handling wastes, and "capable" and "adequately" trained site operators.[29]

A Party must also take "such steps as are necessary" to prevent pollution due to hazardous and other waste management, and must reduce the transboundary movement of waste "to the minimum consistent with the environmentally sound *and efficient* management of such wastes".[30] There is no guidance on what is meant by "minimum," "efficient" or "necessary," and, as indicated above, precious little with regard to "environmentally sound management".

Under Article 4(4), each Party must take "appropriate" legal, administrative and other action to implement and enforce the Convention, including punishing misconduct. Again, there is little indication what this obligation might entail.

In contrast, the trade in wastes of a Party with a non-Party is subject to an obligation which appears reasonably definitive on the surface. Pursuant to Article 4(5), wastes covered by Basel shall not be exported to nor imported from a non-Party. A Party normally may not ship wastes as defined in Basel to a non-Party even if the latter has state-of-the-art disposal facilities.[31] But even here there is disturbing ambiguity. As noted above, the exporting State can extend the scope of "wastes" beyond those listed in the Convention, quite apart from the uncertainty surrounding the definition of household wastes also outlined previously. The fact is that Basel not only treats non-Parties on a discriminatory manner (which might be defendable), but it also fails to provide specific enough guidance to prevent a Party from distorting the Convention's provisions well beyond the likely intent of negotiators in a manner potentially detrimental to non-Parties and other Parties alike.

The Convention on the International Trade in Endangered Species of Wild Fauna and Flora (CITES)

CITES is a primary international instrument for protecting flora and fauna from possible extinction. It tries to do so by providing for the monitoring and regulating of cross-border trade. CITES was done in 1973, entering into force two years later. Currently, there are 115 Parties to this Convention, making it by far the most important of all international wildlife treaties. CITES covers over 20,000 species of plants and more than 500 animal species.[32]

Briefly, the CITES control system is as follows. The Convention divides controlled fauna and flora into three categories (each with a specific detailed Appendix):

- species threatened with extinction (trade in these species and their recognizable parts or derivatives is authorized only under exceptional circumstances);
- species that may become endangered unless trade is regulated; and
- species that an individual Party identifies as being subject to regulation within its own jurisdiction for the purpose of preventing or restricting exploitation, and needing the cooperation of other Parties through the control of trade.

Species are added to one Appendix or another through a regular amending procedure, usually undertaken at a conference of the Parties held every two years or so. More generally, the Parties are obligated to establish a trade control system based on permits and certificates to implement appropriate domestic enforcement measures (including penalties for trade in or possession of specimens traded in violation of the Convention), and to provide regular detailed reports to the CITES Secretariat on cross-border traffic in endangered species and on legislative, regulatory and other measures taken to enforce the provisions of the Convention.[33]

The use of detailed lists of endangered species provides considerable precision as to the scope of the obligations under CITES. Moreover, over the years the Parties have gradually increased the precision of a number of important definitions. For example, pursuant to Article VII specimens of an animal species bred in captivity or a plant species artificially propagated for commercial purposes shall be deemed to be specimens included in Appendix II even if listed in Appendix I (and thus only the authorization of the exporting State can normally be required by the importing State). The key terms were well defined during the Parties' second Conference in 1979, while the procedures for identifying and registering *bona fide* commercial captive-breeding operations have been considerably tightened, establishing an active role for the Secretariat and other Parties.[34] Nonetheless, ambiguities remain. Even more importantly, several provisions, though reasonably clear, can and have given rise to disputes. A few examples should suffice.

Trade in species threatened with extinction (listed in Appendix I of CITES) may occur only if the designated authorities of both the exporting *and* importing states specify that trading the specimen in question "will not be detrimental to the survival of that species".[35] Disagreements can arise in this regard. One recent high profile case relates to the decision taken by Parties in 1989 (not unanimous) to move the African elephant from the regulated list (Appendix II) to the list covering species threatened with extinction (Appendix I). This change led to a ban by most CITES members on imports of African elephant ivory over the objections of several African countries. These included Zimbabwe, which claimed, with some justification, that its practice of controlled harvesting actually had co-existed with an *increase* in its elephant population and, therefore, that regulated trade in ivory should continue as it was not detrimental to the survival of its African elephant population. The 1989 Conference of Parties established a Panel of Experts to undertake a case-by-case review, but its recommendations were not to be binding. Parties would simply "take into account the report of the Panel".[36] A more formal review mechanism leading to the resolution of the dispute based on the Panel's factual findings and recommendations would have been helpful in managing this matter.

A different problem arises with regard to regulated species (i.e., those listed in Appendix II). For a specimen in this category, the exporting country's authorities have the primary responsibility. They can issue an export permit if satisfied, *inter alia*, that such trade will not be detrimental to the survival of a particular species. The importing country must normally accept the presentation of a duly issued export permit as sufficient evidence that the transaction is consistent with the obligations of the Convention. A problem here is that an importing country might believe that an exporting country is unduly limiting exports needed for a local processing industry (to take one example). The exporting country authorities might draw on Article IV(3) which mandates limitations "in order to maintain that species throughout its range at a level *consistent with its role in the ecosystems* in which it occurs and *well above the level* at which that species *might* become eligible for inclusion in Appendix I..." (emphasis added). There is scope for disagreement here, given the ambiguity of the key concepts.[37]

To take one final example of a potential problem, Article XIV provides very broad, ill-defined authority that essentially allows any Party to adopt stricter domestic measures unilaterally than allowed under the Convention to regulate the "trade, taking, possession, or transport of species" whether or not listed in one of the three Appendices. To the degree that this provision is aimed at strengthening the domestic regime on domestic species it is likely unobjectionable in practice. Implicitly, however, this provision also includes the extraordinary authority to implement a complete prohibition of imports of a species, its parts and derivatives orginating in another Party—i.e., the authority to act extraterritorially. Presumably, a country so exercising its right under this provision would justify its action by claiming that the species in question was in some way endangered in another Party.[38] At present, the resolution of a dispute arising in this regard would have to be addressed elsewhere, likely under a trade agreement such as the GATT, because the CITES, as we shall see below, does not have a well-elaborated dispute settlement system.

With respect to non-Parties, differences in treatment have gradually entered the CITES system. Pursuant to Article XIV, stricter trade measures (if a member State believes that trade threatens the survival of a species) are encouraged, "particularly when... trade with a non-Party is involved...". Parties may allow imports from a non-Party of captive-bred and artifically propagated specimens of Appendix I species only after receiving favourable advice from the Secretariat (the latter's role is less sweeping with regard to such trade among Parties).[39]

Finally, in closing this section, it is worth noting that member countries recognize that, quite apart from possible differences in interpretation, there are real enforcement problems associated with CITES. For example, a recent U.S.publication reproduced the following refreshingly straight-forward evaluation of the U.S. Fish and Wildlife Service:

Computerized cargo is of such volume into the United States that only a very small percentage of containers entering the United States is inspected for violations. We suspect large amounts of illegal trade goes undetected.[40]

Technically, this puts the U.S. in violation of its obligations to penalize trade in or possession of specimens of endangered species.[41] The U.S. is by no means alone in this regard. The periodic Conferences of the Parties regularly approve resolutions that refer to serious, widespread difficulties related to compliance matters.

DISPUTE SETTLEMENT: ON GEESE AND GANDERS

MORE THAN ONE-THIRD OF EXISTING INTERNATIONAL environmental agreements contain dispute settlement provisions.[42] Such mechanisms are becoming a normal part of IEAs. This is entirely appropriate and necessary. Yet compared to trade agreements, the dispute settlement provisions in IEAs remain underdeveloped. Given the much longer history of negotiating trade agreements, this difference is understandable, but nonetheless serious.

The Montreal Protocol

The possible exceptions to disciplines listed above not only highlight cracks in the control system not open to non-Parties. Several could also lead to disputes among Parties. This consideration leads to the second stage in this commentary on the Montreal Protocol. There may well be disputes about exemptions, about outright cheating, about Parties who might attempt to meet their consumption reduction targets by putting a more than proportional burden on imports (from other Parties) compared to domestic production, and so forth.

The ultimate test of fairness in terms of the letter of an international agreement is two-fold. First, whether the disciplines are as tight on Parties as they are on non-Parties. We have seen that, to some degree, this is not so and that, in any event, the Protocol places Parties acting jointly in the position of deciding whether to accept a non-Party's good faith efforts. Second, fairness rests in the discipline wielded by member countries against a wayward Party.

In this latter regard, the Protocol and the Vienna Convention leave much to be desired. Under the Convention, the Party complained against can effectively block all progress. First comes negotiation among interested parties, then the use of good offices or third party mediation. A member State may agree to binding arbitration or resolution by the International Court of Justice, but only if it chooses to do so. Even if a member State declares upon ratifying the Convention that it will accept arbitration if challenged, the language contains the caveat "for a dispute not resolved" through negotiation, good offices or mediation. Any party to a dispute can simply claim that one of these processes has not finished (there are no time limits established).[43] And even if Parties go to "binding" arbitration, any controversy as regards the interpretation or manner of implementation of the arbitral tribunal's award may only be submitted back to the tribunal. That is, at the end of the day, the arbitral process has no teeth. Nor does the last option under the Convention: the establishment of a conciliation commission charged with making recommendations "which the parties shall consider in good faith." Hardly a weighty stick.[44]

The Montreal Protocol dispute settlement provision is Article 8, which is just over three lines long. Clearly, the successful disciplining of Parties was not foremost in the minds of the negotiators in 1987. Over the next several years, considerable thought was given to how to structure an appropriate dispute resolution system, culminating with some modest success in 1992 in Copenhagen. The agreed non-compliance procedure establishes an Implementation Committee of ten Parties whose main task is to seek "amicable" solutions to disputes. However, the Committee must report to the Meeting of Parties, including with any appropriate recommendations.[45] The Parties "may ... decide upon and call for steps to bring about full compliance...."[46] None of these procedures has any time limits established. Despite the formal voting requirements, the tradition in the Meeting of Parties is to decide everything by consensus. This *de facto* rule does not facilitate the search for discipline on the Parties.

But what if a Meeting of the Parties does decide to act? What measures might be taken? In Copenhagen, Parties agreed to a carrot and stick approach. Appropriate technical or other assistance could be offered on the one hand. On the other, Parties could issue "cautions," or suspend specific rights and privileges under the Protocol including financial, technical, and institutional benefits, as well as the right to partial exemptions from production and consumption targets and trade-related privileges - the latter left undefined but presumably covering such items as the non-inclusion of recycled imports and exports when calculating domestic "consumption" for purposes of reaching reduction targets.[47] One aspect seems clear. Parties whose rights and privileges might be suspended (and the prospect in practice is very remote), nonetheless remain Parties, and not subject to the trade restrictions imposed on non-Parties pursuant to Article 4. In contrast, non-Parties are presumed guilty and have their trade with Parties unilaterally determined by the terms of the Protocol.

The Basel Convention

As discussed above, many of Basel's obligations are unclearly drafted. For a non-Party, of course, Basel represents a kind of automatic dispute settlement system whereby, ambiguities in drafting aside, a non-Party is, in a sense, presumed guilty by the mere fact of being a non-Party. Such a country is thus condemned to a trade ban in hazardous and certain other wastes regardless of how responsible a non-Party might be in practice with respect to the handling of such wastes and of its economic interests in the matter.

Parties are *not* subject to an equally definitive dispute settlement process. Pursuant to Article 16(1), the Basel Secretariat can prepare reports, including on the implementation of obligations. Presumably, a report could include commentary critical of a Party's enforcement of the Convention's obligations. Such a report, if published or otherwise made available, could increase the public pressure on a government to mend its ways.

However, if a Party believes that another country is acting in breach of its obligations, and that the public spotlight provided by a Secretariat report is insufficient, it can also attempt to settle the matter through negotiation.[48] If this fails and if all the parties to the dispute agree, then the matter can be submitted to the International Court of Justice or to arbitration. Note that the Party complained against must agree to pursue either of these options and thus retains a veto, in practice, over the process. But even if all those concerned agree to submit the dispute to arbitration, the process remains the hostage of the country complained against. The finding or award of an *ad hoc* arbitral tribunal is supposed to be "final and binding" under Basel. Nonetheless, there is no mechanism for ensuring that the award will, in fact, be implemented. There is no sanction to discipline a Party that fails to act on the award. Any dispute on the award's interpretation or execution may merely be referred back to the original *ad hoc* arbitral tribunal or to another tribunal constituted for such purpose.[49] The Party complained against can simply dig in and frustrate further action, while the complaining Party is not authorized under the Convention (much less under the GATT) to impose a sanction.

Thus, we could face the anomalous situation in which a highly responsible non-Party functioning on a best practice basis is faced with a trade ban on certain materials justified under Basel by a Party than unilaterally expands the scope of the Convention to cover waste or scrap material about which there is no consensus internationally as to its hazardous nature. On the other hand, this same Party may be challenged by another signatory about the former's failure to manage the same material in an environmentally sound manner and that Party could, with impunity, refuse arbitration or refuse to implement properly an adverse arbitral ruling. For its part, the 1992 OECD Council Decision on the transfrontier movement of wastes destined for recovery operations contains no dispute settlement provisions.[50]

CITES

As discussed above, a comprehensive CITES mechanism for resolving differences effectively is necessary. Current provisions are inadequate. The Convention's Secretariat, if satisfied that an endangered species is threatened by trade in specimens of that species or that the provisions of the Convention are not being effectively implemented, must notify a designated authority of the country in question. In response, that Party must provide relevant information and *may* hold an inquiry ("expressly authorized by the Party"). The information provided and the results of any inquiry must be reviewed by the next Conference of Parties to CITES which *may* make recommendations for further action.[51] The information produced by this process would usually become public, generating pressure for remedial action.

Overall, a negotiated outcome is clearly preferred. There are notification and consultation commitments. The CITES Secretariat has a "good offices" role in trying to solve problems.[52] If a solution is not found (as defined by either Party to the dispute), the Parties *may, by mutual consent,* submit the dispute to arbitration. In such a case, the arbitral decision is to be binding (but there is no follow-up mechanism to ensure that it is).[53]

A 1992 Resolution of the Parties highlights the importance of establishing a comprehensive dispute settlement mechanism. In order to ensure that trade in Appendix II fauna does not become detrimental to the survival of a particular species, the Animals Committee of CITES is directed to monitor such trade and make corrective recommendations. The Secretariat communicates these to the Party concerned, which must "satisfy" the Secretariat within a specific time period that it has taken action to implement the recommendations. If the Secretariat is not satisfied, it refers the matter to the Standing Committee of the Parties (comprising a representative number of signatories) which may recommend to other Parties that they take "strict measures, including as appropriate suspension of trade in the affected species..." with the Party complained against. In one sense, this Resolution is a hopeful sign that signatories have begun to flesh out what is, in practice, a more elaborate dispute settlement process. Yet critical procedural balances are missing (e.g., the method of choosing members of the Animals Committee, the lack of rules of procedure, etc.). More work in this regard is required.[54]

SANCTIONS: ON LIMITATIONS AND OPTIONS

SANCTIONS HAVE LONG BEEN PART of the foreign policy environment. Questions related to their effectiveness and appropriateness are not well-understood (there is a surprisingly limited literature on the subject). For all players, especially small and medium-sized countries, the use of sanctions merits close attention because such mechanisms can be abused by major powers acting unilaterally for geo-political reasons or in response to domestic special interest groups (e.g., representing environmental, commercial, ethnic, human rights or other concerns). Yet a dispute settlement system *without* provision for sanctions at the end of the road is widely perceived (probably correctly) as lacking credibility.

Ideally, a sanctions provision will do its job without ever being used—the deterrence effect will be sufficient. The sanction need not be unleashed. Nonetheless, the achievement of this happy scenario requires a credible sanction—one that could work to change the behaviour of another, recalcitrant country if ever used.

A recent Policy Staff Paper identified several preconditions that should be met when developing a credible sanctions mechanism.[55] First, unilateralism undermines the cooperative work that must lie at the heart of civilized international behaviour. Unilateralism reflects failure; a serious breakdown in the system of international relations. Second, and flowing from the first precondition, we should work to develop a sanctions mechanism that attracts the broadest possible international support. Moreover, such broad consensus is likely necessary if countries are to perceive sanctions as potentially effective. Third, the burden of sanctions among countries taking such a measure should be equitably distributed. Fourth, the level of the sanction should be adapted to the nature and extent of the fault. Proportionality is important. Fifth, the impact of sanctions on the target country should be carefully evaluated. Will the sanction induce improved behaviour or simply encourage greater recalcitrance? This in turn will depend in part on the level of behaviour of the countries imposing the sanction (e.g., are signatories to an Agreement living up to its obligations?). Finally, sanctions should be seen as only part of the solution. Sanctions alone are unlikely to change State behaviour.

Having recognized the limited utility of sanctions in practice as well as the importance of sanctions as a signal that governments are serious about certain international obligations, there are many options that governments can marshall. Here there is an interesting question. Much of the debate on the enforcement of environmental agreements has focussed on the use of trade sanctions. For example, the U.S. vigorously sought the inclusion of trade sanctions in the recent NAFTA side agreement negotiations to provide the ultimate discipline on Mexican, U.S. and Canadian commitments to effectively enforce domestic environmental and labour law.[56] The fact that the use of trade sanctions invariably favours the largest, but least trade dependent economy (the U.S. in the NAFTA case) was not lost on the Canadian negotiators.

Yet the menu of possible sanctions is, in fact, quite extensive. A recent study provides a list of diplomatic, political, cultural, financial, commercial and technical assistance-related options covering a full three pages.[57]

In a decision taken in the 1992 Meeting of the Parties of the Montreal Protocol, a useful fleshing out occurred of measures that *might* be taken (by Parties as a group—*not* unilaterally) when a country has not been complying with its obligations under the Protocol.[58] Options identified include positive actions, such as technology transfer, financial assistance, and assistance to facilitate data collection and reporting—all with a view to encouraging non-complying Parties (especially LDCs) to meet the challenges in reducing consumption of ozone depleting substances. On the "disciplinary" side, a Meeting of the Parties could issue formal cautions (presumably with accompanying publicity). In addition, they could suspend specific rights and obligations under the Protocol, including the right to vote, the right to exclude the use of recycled or used substances for the purpose of calculating consumption reductions, the right of a Party to transfer to another Party a portion of its calculated level of production of ozone depleting substances, or the right of an LDC Party to concessional financing to meet compliance adjustment costs under the Protocol's Multilateral Fund.

For its part, the North American Agreement on Environmental Cooperation introduces the concept of fines (euphemistically called "monetary enforcement assessments") as the primary penalty waiting at the end of a carefully crafted dispute settlement mechanism meant to address a Party's persistent pattern to effectively enforce its environmental law.[59] In face of a U.S. or Mexican failure to pay such a monetary assessment, another Party may ultimately suspend NAFTA (i.e., trade-related) benefits no greater than the level of the assessment. This twist was not acceptable to Canada for cases when Canadian practice might be found wanting. Instead, Canada agreed to have the fine (a maximum of U.S. $20 million) made enforceable by the three country Commission through the appropriate domestic court in

Canada on a summary proceedings basis not subject to domestic review or appeal.[60] When pressed, creative, non trade-related solutions can be found.

The trade and environment debate over recent years is gradually obliging policy makers to review more carefully the range of positive and disciplinary measures that can be brought into play to strengthen the seriousness with which countries enter into binding international environmental commitments. Clearly, the menu of mechanisms is broader than the narrow focus on trade (and especially trade in goods) initially suggested. This is not to say that trade sanctions should not be contemplated in any circumstance. However, for a trade dependent, medium-sized economy such as Canada, it is somewhat reassuring that the international debate on sanctions is gradually widening to focus on a menu of options. Nonetheless, the necessary link to a well constructed, effective dispute settlement mechanism is still insufficiently understood, much less accepted.

AFTERTHOUGHTS

ONE CRITICAL LITMUS TEST OF HOW THE ENVIRONMENTAL and trade communities have begun to bridge their initial differences is the degree to which both groups can work together to ensure the ultimate compatibility of evolving IEA sanctions with rights and obligations found in other kinds of international agreements. In the case of trade in goods, this means the General Agreement on Tariffs and Trade in the first instance.

Environmentalists, and many others, have legitimate concern. As the comprehensiveness of IEAs continues to evolve, it is disturbing that a non-Party to a particular IEA (the "rogue" State issue) or a Party "in bad standing" might successfully use GATT cover to fight the imposition of a trade sanction currently or eventually deemed necessary under an IEA to ensure that governments do not undermine global commons and other environmental commitments.

On the other hand, many trade policy specialists have a fundamental concern that the possible combination of trade sanctions with loosely drafted obligations and, in particular, the lack of effective compliance provisions including a dispute settlement mechanism creates an environment in which the market and economic power of the few may well prevail over a rules-based system, the latter being the bed-rock of Canadian foreign policy. The "power" approach stacks the deck against Canadian interests.

Many observers are understandably hesitant to exchange the reasonably well developed and effective dispute settlement mechanisms found in modern trade agreements for the lesser discipline of their environmental counterparts until the latter become more sophisticated and effective. This concern is especially important if the policy intent is to ensure that disputes over measures taken to underpin a Party's compliance with an environmental obligation normally be adjudicated under an IEA rather than under a trade agreement. There is considerable merit in such an approach: there *should* be a presumption that a measure (even a trade measure) taken pursuant to an IEA is used to pursue a legitimate environmental objective under the same agreement and, therefore, that disputes in this regard should be resolved by mechanisms established in the IEA. Moreover, a broader range of sanctions could be marshalled under an IEA than under a trade agreement. The key, nonetheless, is whether there is an effective dispute settlement mechanism in place to adjudicate reasonably clear rights and obligations. These issues were directly addressed, with positive results, in the North American Agreement on Environmental Cooperation.

Work is also actively underway internationally (especially in GATT/WTO and OECD committees) to explore the issue of consistency between trade and environmental agreements, as well as other aspects of the trade and environment debate. A few voices state that the GATT as it stands is already sufficiently flexible to accommodate "legitimate" environmental enforcement matters. Nonetheless, most participants accept that some change is likely required, focussing on two approaches:

- the use of the GATT Article XXV:5 right to seek a waiver from certain obligations under the General Agreement (e.g., permitting the use of a discriminatory trade measure against a non-Party to an IEA); or
- any one or combination of adjustments to the general exceptions provision of GATT (Article XX) to accommodate necessary trade measures.[61]

Without engaging in the waiver versus amendment debate in any detail, one particularly innovative technique could be to build further on the so-called "trumping treaty clause" developed by the NAFTA negotiators.[62] Although this trilateral provision clearly does not apply to non-Parties to the NAFTA, it does establish the broad precedence of several IEAs in the case of a conflict between the specific trade obligations of a listed IEA and the NAFTA obligations of Canada, the U.S. and Mexico.[63] This approach has the merit of ensuring a sense of permanency and stability about the exemption created coupled with a review of each IEA when presented for inclusion in the list of exempted agreements.

The criteria to apply in this vetting process lie at the heart of the matter. In light of the concerns raised throughout this Paper, I would suggest that a good candidate IEA for inclusion in a "trumping treaty" provision for global commons or other environmental issues of broad interest should contain several key characteristics. Such an IEA should:

- be open to all countries on equal terms through an accession provision;
- enjoy the support of at least two-thirds of the world's economies responsible for two-thirds of the production and consumption of the substance or good disciplined in the agreement (e.g., Parties to the Montreal Protocol account for more than 90% of world consumption and 99% of world production of halons and certain CFCs);
- contain clearly defined obligations that are at least as onerous on Parties in practice as the standard expected of non-Parties if they were to seek accession;

- feature effective compliance provisions, including a well-constructed dispute settlement mechanism that can, as required, resolve differences in interpretation and discipline a Party found to be acting in a manner inconsistent with its obligations;[64] and
- provide for a range of sanctions against signatories, with a strong preference for including trade sanctions as an instrument of last resort with the right to opt for a different but equally effective tool.

The above criteria are not easy to meet. But then an exemption from normal trade disciplines is not a light matter. The trade policy community must accept that the use of trade sanctions cannot be dismissed out of hand and that we need a practical end to the rather fruitless debate about how broadly based must a broadly based IEA be to qualify for an exemption. Yet, the environmental community has done no-one a service by rushing forward to seek exemptions without first submitting their own handiwork to hard, cold review. The fact is that the clarity and completeness of environmental agreements still fall considerably short of the increasing degree of commitment and sophistication evidenced in trade agreements over the past 20 years. This gap presumably can narrow with time. The final conclusion of this Paper is that both communities must work even more closely together to achieve greater policy coherence by developing high quality international environmental agreements that meet the criteria suggested above.

FOOTNOTES

1. The writer was a member of Canada's NAFTA negotiating team and the lead negotiator for Canada of the North American Agreement on Environmental Cooperation.
2. Annex III, GATT document L/6896 (September 1991). A U.S. government report identified 170 multilateral (global and regional) and bilateral environmental agreements, two-thirds having been signed since 1972. See United States International Trade Commission, *International Agreements to Protect the Environment and Wildlife*, USITC Publication 2351 (January 1991), p. vii.

3. GATT, *International Trade 90-91,* Vol. I (Geneva 1992), pp. 24-5.
4. *Ibid.,* p. 35.
5. The Convention is reproduced in Ozone Secretariat, *Handbook for the Montreal Protocol on Substances that Deplete the Ozone Layer,* 3rd edition (August 1993), Annex XX, pp. 128-49, and Annex XXI, pp. 150-9).
6. See Decision 3, in *Handbook,* p.136, note 11.
7. See the Decisions made in all four Meetings of the Parties, *Handbook,* pp. 29-57.
8. The dates range from a January 1990 start-up of the ban on imports of certain CFCs and halons from non-Parties, to January 1995 for two-way trade in hydrobromofluorocarbons.
9. Annex D to the Protocol, *Handbook,* p. 28.
10. See Articles 4.4, 4.4bis, 4.4ter.
11. See Decisions IV/17B and IV/17C, *Handbook,* pp. 37-8. In the November 1993 Bangkok Meeting, the Parties decided to extend this grace period for one more year for just four non-Parties: Turkey, Poland, Malta and Jordan.
12. See Articles 1.5 and 1.6 plus Decision IV/24, *Handbook,* pp. 5, 32. Note that recycled material is excluded from the control structure because it can be re-introduced without the release of harmful material to the environment, while chemicals used as feedstock are, it is felt, completely used or contained in the production process and therefore do not affect the environment. Nonetheless, the point is that trade in these contexts is not permitted with non-Parties, except as agreed pursuant to Article 4.8.
13. Article 2B.2.
14. Articles 2A.4, 2B.2, 2C.3, 2D.2, 2E.3, 2G.1
15. The agreed definition of "essential" is not narrowly drafted - see Decision IV/24, *Handbook,* pp. 35-6. In the November 1993 Bangkok Meeting, the Parties decided that there was no justification for granting halon production/consumption exemptions for 1994.
16. Article 5.1; Decisions I/12E and III/3(d), *Handbook,* pp. 38-9.
17. Articles 5.6, 5.9, 10 and 10A.
18. For example, between 1986 and 1988, 3.5 million tonnes of hazardous wastes were shipped to developing countries—see UNEP/CHW.1/24, paragraph 8.
19. The U.S. implementing legislation has been stuck in Congress.
20. Article 1(1)(b), in UNEP/IG.80/3 of March 22, 1989.
21. OECD,C(92) 39/FINAL, adopted March 30, 1992—see Annex 1, Section II(2) and Appendices 3 and 4.
22. See also UNEP/CHW.1/24, Annex II, Decision I/9, pp. 27-8 for a related decision by the Parties to Basel.
23. OECD,C(92) 39/FINAL, Annex 1, Section II (6), and Appendix 4, 3rd footnote.

24. Ibid., Annex 1, Section IV, Case (1)(c) and Case (2) (d).
25. See "Framework Document and Technical Guidelines," Na. 93-7758/190793, p. 51, paragraphs 4-5, 8-9.
26. Article 4(2)(b).
27. Moreover, pursuant to Article 4(8): "Each Party shall require that hazardous wastes or other wastes, to be exported, are managed in an environmentally sound manner in the State of import or elsewhere."
28. Article 2(8) tries unsuccessfully to define the phrase through vague references to "all practicable steps" and to protecting human health *and the environment* "against the adverse effects which may result".
29. See "Framework Document and Technical Guidelines," p. 5, paragraph 9. See also the interesting comments made by several developing countries, the Nordics and the Greenpeace observer pushing for a mandatory ban on all hazardous waste exports to LDCs even for recycling purposes and even if the importing country wanted to engage in this business and possessed the proper disposal facilities (in UNEP/CHW.1/24, Annex IV). Sending this kind of market signal could make it less likely that certain developing countries attract world class disposal facilities.
30. Articles 4(2)(c) and (d).
31. Although, pursuant to Article 11, a Party "may" enter into a bilateral or other arrangement with a non-Party that would allow such trade, as long as the arrangement is fully consistent with the environmentally sound management (whatever that is!) required by Basel. However, nothing obliges a Party to enter into such an arrangement.
32. USITC, *International Agreements,* p. 5-29.
33. See CITES, Articles VI and VII.
34. Resolutions Conf. 2.12, 6.21 and 8.15. Other useful definitional work includes Resolutions Conf. 2.14, 3.15, 4.10, 4.11, 5.10, 5.16 and 8.17.
35. CITES, Article III.
36. Resolution Conf. 7.9.
37. The reverse problem is now subject to tighter international review. The Animals Committee of CITES was empowered in 1992 to monitor whether exports of specimens of a particular animal species are becoming detrimental to that species' survival. If so, the Committee can recommend corrective measures which, if not implemented, can lead to the suspension of trade with that Party in the affected species. See Resolution Conf. 8.9.
38. A close reading of CITES can lead to an even more puzzling scenario. Article XV provides for amending the lists of endangered species, basically by a two-thirds vote. Theoretically, a Party could seek, in response to a domestic lobby, to shift a species found in another country from Appendix II to Appendix I, which would provide the

importing authority with greater scope for trade restrictive action. The proposing Party, however, could fail to achieve the required support from other member countries, and yet *still* choose to prohibit imports of specimens of the species in question by exercising its right under Article XIV. See also Resolution Conf. 6.7 (July 1987).
39. Resolutions Conf. 2.6 and 8.8 respectively. Other examples are found in Resolutions Conf. 4.15 and 5.16(j).
40. Cited in USITC, *International Agreements,* p. 5-29.
41. CITES, Article VIII.
42. OECD, COM/ENV/TD (93)118, 15 November 1993, paragraph 1.
43. Note that the 1991 Protocol on Environmental Protection to the Antarctic Treaty usefully tightens its proceedings by giving Parties to a dispute 12 months to resolve it by consultation, failing which any single party can refer the issue to an arbitral tribunal. The problem of enforcing a tribunal's findings remains. See Protocol Articles 18-20 and the relevant appendix.
44. Vienna Convention, Article 11; Decision I/7, Handbook, pp. 138-40.
45. Approval requires a simple majority vote of those present and voting—see Rule 26.6(b) of the Rules of Procedure, in *Handbook,* p. 165.
46. This requires a two-thirds majority of those present and voting—see Rule 40.1 of the Rules of Procedures, in *Handbook,* p. 167.
47. Various Decisions, *Handbook,* pp. 46-9, Annexes VII and VIII of *Handbook,* pp.81-3.
48. See Articles 19 and 20(1).
49. See Articles 20(2) and (3), and Annex VI of the Basel Convention. Note that Article 20(3) also allows a Party to declare in advance that it accepts the arbitration and/or ICJ alternatives in relation to any other Party accepting the same obligations. The ultimate problem remains on how to ensure the implementation of any award.
50. Apart from a shadowy reference to cooperation found in Annex 1, Section VI(4).
51. CITES, Article XIII.
52. For example, see respectively Conf. 6.7 (July 1987) and Resolution Conf. 7.5 (October 1989).
53. CITES, Article XVIII. This Article, entitled "Resolution of Disputes," comprises two brief paragraphs covering just seven lines of text.
54. Resolution Conf. 8.9.
55. Jean Prévost, *Pour des sanctions efficaces et appropriées,* Document du Groupe des Politiques, No. 93/4 (mars 1993), pp. 3-4, 49-54.
56. See the "North American Agreement on Environmental Cooperation," Final Draft, September 13, 1993.
57. Prévost, *Pour des sanctions,* pp. 36-8.
58. See Decisions IV/5 and Annex VII, *Handlbook,* pp. 48-9, 83.
59. See "North American Agreement," Part Five, and particularly

Articles 34-36 and Annexes 36A and 36B. Of course, the environmental side agreement does *not* address the matter of sanctions against non-Parties.
60. *Ibid.*, Annex 36A. Note that the Maastricht Treaty provides (in Article 171(2)) for fines to be imposed by the European Commission if Member States fail to implement judgements of the European Court of Justice. This provision applies, *inter alia,* to environmental laws and regulations at the Community level.
61. Note that the Agreement to establish the World Trade Organization entered into force in January 1995 and covers, *inter alia,* both goods and services. Article IX of this Agreement provides for a *waiver* if approved by three-fourths of the Members. This is a higher threshold than the previous GATT rule requiring the approval of two-thirds of the votes cast. Article X provides for *amendments* that shall take effect for the Members that have accepted them upon acceptance by two-thirds of the Members. This tracks the former GATT amending formula.
62. See Article 104 of the NAFTA.
63. The IEAs are the Montreal Protocol, the Basel Convention and CITES. Note that the "trumping" feature relates to *mandatory* trade provisions requiring a Party to take a certain course of action, provided that where a Party has a choice among equally effective and reasonably available means of complying with such obligations (e.g., seeking arbitration on questions of science related to environmentally sound practice), the alternative that is least inconsistent with the NAFTA shall be chosen.
64. Again, this feature is critical if the IEA is to be more fully "trumping," i.e., so that a dispute involving a trade measure taken against a Party might normally be heard under an IEA, rather than under a trade agreement (which is still the case with NAFTA Article 104).

III

Robert T. Stranks

Pandora's Box?: Countervailing Duties and the Environment

Indeed, the subsidies question in relation to environmental policies may be one of the most intricate and difficult of those facing the world trading system during the next decade. John Jackson, "World Trade Rules and Environmental Policies: Congruence or Conflict?"

INTRODUCTION

THIS PAPER MAKES SOME OBSERVATIONS and raises several questions on the trade-environment policy interface. Environmental considerations are having an increasingly important role in shaping the international trading system. In a general sense, the Paper gives a positive response to the broad question of whether environmental objectives can be attained without destroying the GATT/WTO. Trade measures are already included in a number of International Environmental Agreements, and the GATT allows for the use of nondiscriminatory market access restrictions to protect a country's environment.[1] The question of whether the GATT should allow for the use of trade measures in response to environmental degradation in foreign countries remains. Is there a certain range of circumstances when multilaterally agreed trade measures could potentially play an environmental role? This Paper raises some questions on the possible application of trade measures, specifically what may be considered a *new* form of countervailing duty, for environmental reasons. The issues raised are complex and more than occasionally politicized. Our analysis indicates that the likelihood of developing a new and *effective* form of countervailing-like duties to address subsidization with adverse environmental affects is problematical.

There has been little constructive international dialogue on revising multilateral trade rules to allow for the use of countervailing-like duties to take into account environmental concerns more fully. To the limited extent that there has been a discussion, it has been polarized, with some environmental groups arguing for a broad application of countervailing-like duties, and the trade policy community holding the view that such environmentally related duties are undesirable and would have adverse implications for the international trading system. One commentator, reflecting the environmentalist view, has concluded that "it is an anachronism that at a time when people are focusing on changing development practices to make them sustainable, the trading community is forbidding the use of trade measures to assist in this process."² For each group, their respective view rests on serious concern about very real public policy issues.³

Fundamental questions of what may be the acceptable scope or criteria for introducing countervailing-like duties on environmental grounds, and the practical problems with using such an instrument to encourage a change in a foreign country's policies, have not been fully explored. One important question that we will address more fully in this Paper is: should generally available subsidies, with the important caveat that there is a significant environmental impact⁴, be candidates for countervailing-like duties? The key notion of the question is that of applying a trade instrument to encourage adjustment of subsidization practices that have detrimental environmental effects *and* affect a tradable good.

ENVIRONMENTAL CONCERNS

THERE APPEARS TO BE BROAD AGREEMENT that subsidies may contribute to environmental degradation.⁵ A recent World Bank report stated that: "Some government polices are downright harmful for the environment. Notable here are distorted prices in general and subsidized input prices in particular."⁶ A key message of the report was the importance of removing subsidies that encourage excessive use of fossil fuels, irrigation water, pesticides and logging. The report noted that the removal of all energy subsidies, including those on coal in the industrialized countries, would sharply reduce local pollution and cut global carbon emissions from energy by 10 per cent.⁷

Anecdotal evidence indicates that many governments underprice natural resources. Figure 1 presents some data on the ratio of user prices to production costs for some energy and agricultural inputs. From this data, it is evident that many users pay less than the production costs of natural resource inputs. In Mexico, farmers pay only 20 per cent of the production cost of irrigation water. In the U.S., to give another example, it has been estimated that the Bureau of

Figure 1
Ratio of Price to Production Cost, Selected Energy and Agricultural Inputs

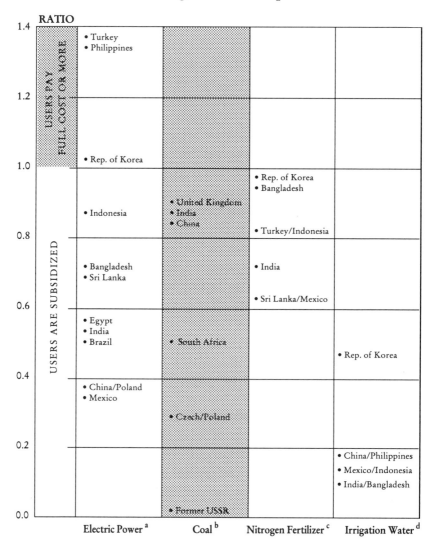

a. Average electricity tariff as a proportion of the incremental cost of system expansion (1987; Egypt 1991).
b. Domestic price as a proportion of border price or long-run marginal cost (various years, 1987-91, except South Africa, 1982).
c. Farmgate price of urea as a proportion of the average production cost of urea (average of various years, 1980-88).
d. Direct water charge as a proportion of operating and maintenance costs plus midrange estimate of annualized capital cost (various years, 1985-88).

Sources: World Bank, World Bank Development Report 1992, p.69.

Reclamation provides a subsidy to the farms that use its water of over U.S. $1 billion per year.[8] The underpricing of timber rights (i.e., below replacement cost) may encourage excessive logging. The World Bank has reported that, in a sample of African countries, timber stumpage fees constitute only a small percentage (less than five per cent in the cases of Niger, Senegal and Sudan) of the replacement costs.[9] Higher input costs, such as for energy, are also likely to stimulate interest in more efficient production processes, with corresponding environmental benefits.[10] Both the World Bank and the International Monetary Fund are increasingly trying to encourage countries receiving financing, such as for electric power projects, to adopt more environmentally (and economically) sound pricing policies.[11] There is a clear need for extensive empirical case studies on how natural resource pricing practices may contribute to environmental degradation.[12]

It is clear that, in several circumstances, increases in resource-user charges, such as for water and forests, may support environmental objectives. For example, the underpricing of water could result in excessive use, which in the long-term could result in the loss or reduced productivity of land due to salinization or waterlogging.[13] Subsidies, by lowering costs to producers, may contribute to market failure and the accompanying negative environmental effects. The reduction of direct subsidies would comprise a step toward the fuller internalization of environmental costs.

If natural resources are underpriced, trade and trade liberalization may have an adverse environmental impact. This, however, does not imply that trade or trade liberalization should be avoided, nor that trade measures are the most appropriate response to subsidization of resource use. Rather, as a first best solution, an appropriate domestic environmental policy, crafted to internalize environmental costs, is required to avoid negative environmental impacts. The removal of local price distortions would be of benefit to the environment. Nonetheless, could trade measures play a useful supporting role? More specifically, could environmental countervail-like duties encourage a country to move toward internalizing its environmental costs by adjusting its resource pricing policy?

SUBSIDIES AND COUNTERVAILING DUTIES

THE CURRENT GATT RIGHTS AND OBLIGATIONS for subsidies and countervailing duties are contained in GATT Articles VI and XVI, as well as the Agreement on Interpretation and Application of Articles VI, XVI, and XXIII of the GATT (the Subsidies Code). With the entry into force of the World Trade Organization (WTO) in 1995, the current Subsidies Code, which does not apply to all contracting parties, will be replaced by the Agreement on Subsidies and Countervailing Measures, which will apply to all WTO members.[14]

Countervailing duties are an exception to the general GATT obligation not to increase trade restrictions. Article II of the GATT obliges each party not to impose customs duties in excess of the level listed on its respective tariff schedule. Article VI defines "countervailing duty" as a special duty levied for the purpose of off-setting any subsidy bestowed directly or indirectly upon the manufacture, production or export of any specific merchandise.[15]

Countervailing duties are intended to provide an offset to domestic producers when the producers are experiencing economic injury as a result of a foreign country's provision of targeted subsidies to its domestic producers who subsequently market their goods abroad. Under the rules of the WTO, in order to impose countervailing duties a country must determine that subsidization has occurred in the foreign country, and that the subsidization is causing, or threatening to cause, material injury to domestic producers of the like product, or is retarding the establishment of a domestic industry in the country of importation.

Multilateral trade rules draw a critical distinction between "generally available" and "specific" subsidies, and treat each type of subsidy differently. If a subsidy is "generally available," it is not countervailable. Conversely, if a subsidy is "specific" i.e., confined in law, regulation or practice to an enterprise or industry or group of enterprises or industries within the jurisdiction of the granting authority, it is not excluded from potential countervail action.[16]

Countervailing-Like Duties and the Environment

To pose the question of whether subsidies, in a broader sense that goes beyond the current WTO definition of actionable subsidies, should be countervailable is not to suggest accepting the holus-bolus use of countervailing duties to compensate for differences in countries' environmental standards that reflect different environmental conditions or inevitable disagreements over the nature of the environmental threat or local environmental priorities. This Paper does not suggest that tariffs or other trade measures be put into place to alter competitive positions arising from differences in environmental standards or compliance costs *per se.* There is no suggestion that countervailing-like duties be used for the extraterritorial enforcement elsewhere of one country's domestic standards or to equalize prices on the basis of the cost structure of exploiting the resource in the country contemplating the use of such a measure. This dangerous view that there should be such compensating tariffs—"levelling the playing field"—has been put forth elsewhere.[17]

Varying production costs or environmental standards, either of which may differ across jurisdictions depending on the characteristics of local eco-systems, are not and should not be the basis for applying countervailing-like duties, nor is there a strong case for fully harmonizing environmental policies, as countries are at various levels of economic development, have distinct assimilative capacities and have different social preferences on environmental issues.[18]

Rather, this Paper raises the issue of whether below replacement cost practices with respect to renewable resources or below production cost practices with regard to such non-renewable resources as coal that have a negative environmental impact should be considered countervailable.[19] If a country does not subsidize production, but production or replacement costs of a particular traded good were nonetheless lower than those of its trading partners, there would clearly be no basis for taking trade remedy or any other trade-based action.

Differences in countries' resource pricing, environmental regulations and policies can affect the competitiveness of their domestic producers. A popular public view is that, if foreign producers have lower environmental standards, imports from these producers constitute "social dumping," and that there should be some provision for imposing countervailing duties. But it is obvious that many, perhaps all, government policies, at least indirectly influence competitiveness. Many "benefits" conferred by governments, i.e., roads, education, social policies, health care, are not considered a subsidy. A GATT Working Group concluded that: "There are various actions by governments, economic or otherwise, which may provide an advantage to domestic producers, but which have not traditionally been considered subsidies." The question is where the multilateral community desires to draw the line on what is an allowable basis for competition, and which government policies might appropriately be considered countervailable subsidies.[20]

In this regard, and from a certain environmental perspective, the distinction between "generally available" and "specific" subsidies may pose a problem. Both types of subsidies may contribute to environmental degradation and, in this respect, the countervailablity of "generally available" subsidies, in the WTO sense, may appear warranted. This does, however, muddy the trade rules water by introducing an environmental factor into current subsidy/countervail considerations. As noted above, the purpose of the existing countervailing duty rules is to protect domestic producers from unfair import competition that has benefitted from targeted subsidization. On the other hand, a environmentally based countervailing duty, as expressed by some environmental groups, would be an instrument for encouraging another country to adjust its environmental practices (even those not clearly linked to immediate global commons issues, e.g., user charges for water irrigation purposes) and not strictly, or even primarily, an instrument to protect domestic producers in the importing country from economic injury. Such a tool could become subject to manipulation not only by trade protectionists, but also by those who appear to believe that certain countries should have an extraterritorial right to oblige others to accept harmonized standards. Yet, is this seemingly irreconcilable clash of perspectives necessarily the whole story?

The underlying reason to consider penalizing such "generally available" subsidies through a trade action is an environmental one. In this respect, we face several dilemmas. Countries have already reached a consensus, reflected in the current, arduously negotiated multilateral rules, that "generally available" subsidies are *not* countervailable from a trade distorting perspective. In respect of natural resource pricing policies, which are often identified as contributing to environmental degradation, further complexities arise. Natural resource pricing policies include removal rights, such as the right to harvest timber, as well as the sale of raw material inputs. But the *new* WTO Agreement on Subsidies and Countervailing Measures provides an exhaustive definition of subsidy which is based on the concept of a financial contribution which confers a benefit. This definition does *not* appear to include natural resource pricing.[21] Environmentalists, however, apply a broader definition of subsidization. From the environmental viewpoint, the question is how environmental concerns can be accommodated, or where to redraw the line on what constitutes a countervailable subsidy when the appropriate level of environmental effects is exceeded. While this line of reasoning is intuitively attractive from one vantage point, the issue of where the appropriate threshold might lie (10 per cent underpricing? 50 per cent? the same threshold regardless of resource availability or the domestic impact on the environment?) is an extremely complicated question. In sum, the use of a countervailing-like duty for environmental reasons would require fundamental changes to the current trading rules and could be technically difficult to craft.

As a trade dependent country, ever wary of potential protectionist abuses, Canada has strongly supported discipline in the subsidy/countervail area of trade law. Experience with trade rules abuse necessitates a cautious approach to reform. Any potential loosening, unless very carefully crafted and reasoned, could create an instrument for the use of protectionists in Canadian export markets. Any contemplation of change from the existing rules would also require extensive federal-provincial-private sector consultations.

Further Practical Difficulties and Considerations

A range of other relevant issues arise and serve to illustrate the complexity of applying countervailing duties for environmental reasons. Foremost is the question of effectiveness. Would countervailing-like duties encourage another country to adjust its policies or would such duties simply be considered a cost of doing business? For example, if a country's exports are only 5 per cent of total production of a given product, is it reasonable to expect a countervailing type duty placed on exports to prompt policy changes that will affect all production? Or are more punitive measures, i.e., economic sanctions that go beyond countervailing type duties justified on environmental grounds?[22]

As indicated earlier, the issue of environmental effects is problematical. If the environmental effects are primarily local, affecting only the exporting country, should these effects be considered the same as effects which are transborder or global in nature? And when does "local" end and "global" begin, for example, in light of the carbon sink role of forests? Or is the critical difference simply whether the good containing "subsidized" inputs is traded or not? In establishing an environmental criterion, would there be a need to have some form of "environmental injury" test analogous and in addition to the economic injury to producers in the importing country that must be established under current international subsidy rules? In this respect, there is no reason to believe that the extent of detrimental environmental effects is directly related to the value of a subsidy. For example, the production of two firms receiving the same subsidy could have very different environmental effects because of different technologies employed. These types of considerations may make the use of an environmentally related countervail impractical. They certainly require further close and careful analysis.

A significant additional point to reflect on is how restrictions on imports, such as a countervailing-like duty on environmental grounds, would influence producers in the *importing* country, and the environmental effects stemming from this impact. Restricting imports will alter the incentives for domestic producers and may stimulate production. Unless appropriate policies are in place in the importing country, an increase in its production may contribute to environmental degradation. Indeed, countervailing-like duties could lead to an environmentally perverse result in a case where domestic production is environmentally more unsound than the production of the foreign imports, and the imports are restricted. Thus, the criteria for the use of a countervail-like duty for environment-related purposes may need to consider the environmental and subsidy practices in the country seeking to use the trade measure.[23] This could go some way to ensuring that countervail-like duties are more completely directed at an environmental objective. One option would be to allow the countervail of such subsidies only if domestic firms in the importing country in the same sector were not themselves recipients of such subsidies, or to adjust the countervail duty to take into account differences in subsidy programs. Perhaps, for environmental reasons, there could be a case for linking domestic policy adjustment in the importing country to the use of countervailing-like duties.

Some Concluding Thoughts

The questions surrounding what multilateral discipline to apply to natural resource pricing practices, with the caveat that they have adverse environmental effects, are fundamental for the trade-environment interface. Canada has a strong interest in developing a transparent, rule-based trading system that integrates environmental and trade concerns. To date, the subsidy/countervailing duty dimension has not been adequately addressed. The GATT Working Group on Environmental Measures and International Trade did not consider the use of countervailing duties for environmental purposes.[24] Nor was the relationship considered within the context of the Uruguay Round, which did not consider the trade-environment nexus *per se*. Due to the scope of the Round itself, contracting parties thought that the addition of environmental linkages to trade would have further complicated and delayed the conclusion of the very protracted negotiations.

With the conclusion of the Uruguay Round, and the decision for the World Trade Organization to establish a committee on trade and environment, there is an opportunity to consider countervailing-like measures more fully in an environmental context, and to make recommendations on the matter.[25] This said, there should be no illusion about the intensive effort required to address the issue properly. Its intricacies are not yet understood, nor have the views of the major players been well formulated or articulated. The importance of the issue to certain environmental interest groups, however, necessitates that countries engage in a real dialogue on the use of countervailing duties in an environmental context.

Two aspects of environmental countervail policy are likely to give rise to considerable apprehension in the trade policy community and more broadly. These are the related fears of "slippery slopes" and the opening of Pandora's box. First, a clear need arises to prevent the countervailability of certain generally available subsidies, with environmental implications, from becoming a protectionist tool. Well thought-out and circumscribed disciplines would be required. All parties to a negotiation must understand that the underlying objective is for all countries to adopt appropriate *domestic* environmental resource management practices. Secondly, an exception for an environmental countervail does not imply that the definition of a subsidy must be extended to a wider range of social or economic policies. The inclusion of environmental criteria in the use of countervailing duties should not be a step, for example, toward using trade policy instruments to adjust for differences in labour standards. Nonetheless, there are strong pressures in both the U.S. and the EU to use trade measures to address cost differences arising from differences in a broad range of domestic policies. These issues need to be considered on their own merits, but Pandora's box is already being pried open more than many feel comfortable with.

On the other hand, multilateral rules for circumscribed countervail of generally available subsidies, with some multilaterally agreed threshold of environmental effects, could decrease the domestic political pressure for countries, principally those countries with the most active and influential environmental groups, to act unilaterally.[26] If unilateralism were to occur, the smaller, trade-dependent countries might well find themselves under pressure to adopt environmental practices as directed by the larger players. If left unaddressed and unresolved, a country's exports, including Canada's, could be vulnerable to foreign countries' trade actions motivated by protectionist interests as well as environmental considerations.

Leaving immediate trade interests aside, from an environmental perspective the subsidization of resource inputs and the failure to internalize costs may have negative effects and, frankly, comprise bad economic policy as well. More generally, competitive conditions are influenced by environmental factors; and environmentally related problems, such as the over-harvesting of a renewable resource, could contribute to a reduction in a country's competitiveness over the longer term.

This Paper has explored how we might begin to address more methodically one important issue in the trade and environment universe. This Paper has highlighted the complexities of the issues involved and the dangers that such an exercise could be captured by those whose protectionist instincts are as strong if not stronger than their environmental concern. The questions raised pose serious doubt that multilateral agreement could easily be reached on operationalizing countervailing rules to address environmental concerns. More importantly, a high degree of uncertainty exists on whether a new form of countervailing duties would be effective in achieving its environmental objectives. For the time being, until the issues are more fully understood, it would be prudent for governments to resist pressure to employ countervailing-like duties to influence the manner in which foreign countries address environmental concerns. But this prudence should not prevent us from undertaking a careful and exhaustive review of the mechanics of how such a mechanism might be crafted in a trade and environmentally responsible manner.

FOOTNOTES

1. A number of International Environmental Agreements contain trade restrictive measures. These include the Montreal Protocol on Substances that Deplete the Ozone Layer, the Convention on International Trade in Endangered Species of Wild Fauna and Flora (CITES) and the Basel Convention on the Transboundary Movement of Hazardous Wastes. See Keith H. Christie, "Stacking the Deck: Compliance and Dispute Settlement in International Environmental Agreements," Policy Staff Paper No. 93/15, Department of Foreign Affairs and International Trade, December 1993 (included in this volume).
2. Edith Brown Weiss, "Environment and Trade as Partners in Sustainable Development: A Commentary," American Journal of International Law, 86 (1992), p.731.
3. In addition to the Policy Staff paper mentioned in footnote 1, other Policy Staff contributions that have explored how we might bridge the gap in the debate include: "Trade and the Environment: Dialogue of the Deaf or Scope for Cooperation?," by Michael Hart and Sushma Gera (No. 92/11); Section 4 of "Globalization and Public Policy in Canada: In Search of a Paradigm," by Keith Christie (No. 93/01); and "Dangerous Liaisons: The World Trade Organization and the Environmental Agenda," by K. Anne McCaskill (No. 94/14).
4. "Environmental impact" often refers to specific impacts such as increased pollution, harm to ecosystems or depletion of natural resources, as well as indirect impacts that affect the quality of life. See Robert A. Reinstein, "Trade and Environment: Assessing

Environmental Impacts of Trade Measures and Agreements," prepared for the OECD Environment Directorate, November 1993. As countries have diverse views on environmental degradation, reaching multilateral consensus on environmental criteria would be complex in its own right. For example, it could become a particularly daunting task to identify a threshold for subsidization that causes the serious loss of biodiversity.

5. See World Resources Institute, World Resources 1994-95 and UNCTAD, "Sustainable Development," TD/B/40(2)/6, February 1994.
6. World Bank, World Development Report (1992), p. 11.
7. Ibid., p.12.
8. John Proops, Paul Steele, Ece Ozdemiroglu and David Pearce, "The Internalisation of Environmental Costs and Resource Values: A Conceptual Study," UNCTAD/COM/27, November 1993, pp. 9-11.
9. World Bank, World Development Report (1992), p.149.
10. In respect of government regulation of energy pricing, Article 604 of the NAFTA is important. William G. Watson has concluded that: "Two-price systems of the kind that, in the 1970s and early 1980s, kept domestic Canadian energy prices well below the world price and encouraged excessive consumption in this country are all but impossible under the NAFTA." See William G. Watson, "Environmental and Labour Standards in the NAFTA', Commentary No. 57, Toronto: C.D. Howe Institute, 1994, pp. 7-8.
11. The World Bank Annual (1993), p.49, reports that the Bank will be more selective about where it lends and that: "Support will not continue for energy-supply projects where poorly performing public energy enterprises and governments are unwilling to carry out fundamental structural reforms that could significantly improve the ways they do business. To receive new commitments from the Bank, governments should clearly show they are setting up structural incentives that lead to more efficient energy production and use". An UNCTAD report has noted that the World Bank and IMF have made significant progress in taking environmental issues into account in the formulation of structural adjustment programs, but that more needs to be done if such programs are to promote sustainable development adequately. UNCTAD, TD/B/40(2)/6, p.11.
12. This raises another complexity and case-specific factor in the countervail-environment debate. Detailed work on specific causality would be required to ascertain how a country's natural resource policies contribute to environmental degradation.
13. The World Bank's Operational Directive on Environmental Assessment provides that all approved Bank projects that could have significant adverse effects on the environment are subject to environmental assessments. World Bank, World Development Report (1992), p.81.

14. Several provisions in the Agreement on Subsidies and Countervailing Measures grant the developing countries special and differential treatment. For example, de minimis provisions exempt a developing country from countervailing duties when the subsidy level does not exceed 2 per cent of its value; or the volume of the subsidized imports represents less than 4 per cent, and cumulatively among developing countries benefiting from the provision, less than 9 per cent of total imports. Another provision provides that, in effect, the least-developing countries may maintain export subsidies, while other developing countries have eight years from the entry into force of the WTO to phase out such subsidies.
15. Article VI of the GATT1994.
16. The WTO agreement on subsidies also identifies non-actionable (specific) subsidies on which countervailing duties cannot be applied. In the environmental context, payments up to 20 per cent of the cost of adaptation of existing facilities to new environmental laws and requirements, subject to certain conditions, are considered non-actionable subsidies. These conditions are that the facilities to be adapted must have been in existence for at least two years, and that the assistance must be of a one-time, non-recurring nature, and must be available to all firms that are able to adopt the new equipment and/or production processes. The environmentally related payment must also be "directly linked to and proportionate to a firm's planned reductions of nuisances and pollution in nature, and does not cover any manufacturing cost savings which may be achieved," and it must not cover the cost of replacing and operating the assisted investment, which must be fully borne by firms. The WTO Agreement on Agriculture also provides that "payments under environmental programmes" and "infrastructural works associated with environmental programmes," under certain conditions, are exempt from the subsidy reduction commitments in the rest of the agricultural text.
17. The view that tariffs should compensate for differences in environmental costs was put forward by U.S. Senator David Boren. In 1991, Boren introduced a bill entitled the "International Pollution Deterrence Act," which proposed tariffs which reflected the cost that a foreign producer would incur under U.S. standards. The Conference Board, "Understanding European Environmental Regulation," Report Number 1026, 1993, p. 14.
18. The OECD Polluter Pays Principle recognizes these types of differences. The Principle recognizes that: "Differing national environmental standards, for example with regard to the tolerable amount of pollution, are justified by a variety of factors including, among other things, different pollution assimilative capacities of the environment in the present state, different social objectives and priorities attached

to environmental protection and different degrees of industrialization and pollution density." OECD, "Conceptual Framework for PPM Measures," COM/TD/ENV(93)114/REV 2, p.24.
19. In respect to natural resource policies, such policies would first need to be redefined as a subsidy under revised multilateral rules.
20. GATT, Committee on Subsidies and Countervailing Measures, Group of Experts on the Calculation of Subsidy, "Criteria For Distinguishing Subsidies From Other Measures Having a Trade Distorting Effect," Working Paper No. 15, March 1984, p.1.
21. Agreement on Subsidies and Countervailing Measures, Article 1, Definition of a Subsidy. If natural resource pricing were accepted as a form of subsidization in a revised WTO context, severe measurement problems would likely arise. The difference between the government price and a market price may not be known. One author has noted that "it could be argued that the practical difficulties of establishing the market price are so great, and the potential for an incorrect estimate so large, that the toleration of such potential subsidies would produce less distortion in the international economy than would the imposition of countervailing duties based on an inaccurate calculation of market price." See David Scott Nance, "Natural Resource Pricing Policies and the International Trading System," Harvard International Law Journal, Vol.30, 1989, pp.115-6.
22. The effectiveness of economic sanctions and their ability to alter a country's behaviour is dependent upon a wide range of factors in both the sanctioner and target country. See Robert T. Stranks, "Economic Sanctions: Foreign Policy Foil or Folly?," Policy Staff Commentary No.4, Department of Foreign Affairs and International Trade, May 1994. This and other work undertaken by Policy Staff conclude that sanctions are not usually a very effective foreign policy tool.
23. A net subsidy concept was proposed by Canada (MTN.GNG\NG10\W\25) during the Uruguay Round, but did not muster enough support from the other contracting parties for inclusion in the final agreement. Under this concept, the determination of the amount of the subsidy would be based on the difference between the subsidy on imports and the subsidy on the domestic product. The Canadian proposal did not raise the net subsidy concept in an environmental countervail context.
24. The Working Group's agenda comprised the following three issues: trade provisions contained in existing multilateral environmental agreements vis-à-vis GATT principles and provisions; multilateral transparency of national environmental regulations likely to have trade effects; and the trade effects of new packaging and labelling requirements aimed at protecting the environment.

25. The first meeting of the General Council of the WTO will establish a Committee on Trade and Environment open to all members of the WTO. Pending the first meeting of the General Council, it has been agreed that the work of the Committee on Trade and Environment should be carried out by a Sub-Committee of the Preparatory Committee of the World Trade Organization.
26. It is also likely that, in negotiating the rules, a hard look at domestic environmental practices in the countries actively promoting this agenda would be required. This would also appeal to environmental interests.

IV

ANNE McCASKILL

Dangerous Liaisons: The World Trade Organization and the Environmental Agenda

INTRODUCTION

THERE IS LITTLE DEBATE THESE DAYS about the need to address environmental problems in a timely and effective way. In developed and developing countries alike, concerns about pollution, depletion of resources, the threatened extinction of plant and animal species, atmospheric change and problems associated with the disposal of wastes are contributing to a sense of urgency about the environment. As this sense of urgency grows, political pressure is increasing.

Dealing with the root causes of many environmental issues continues to be difficult, however, due to the still widespread reluctance or inability of both developed and developing countries to face the costs involved. There are no easy answers and progress can be slow. As environmental groups and others grow impatient with the pace of progress, attention is being directed to the use of trade restrictions to pursue environmental goals. Trade restrictions, especially those intended to exert pressure on countries considered to have inadequate environmental programmes and standards, are often seen as fast and effective tools for achieving change. They also have appeal for some governments as a high-profile way to respond to political pressures when other solutions to the underlying environmental problem are considered to be too difficult or costly in the short-term. Accompanying the proposals for trade restrictions are calls for amendments to the international trade rules under the General Agreement on Tariffs and Trade (GATT) and the World Trade Organization (WTO), aimed at providing greater flexibility for trade action.

Discussions on trade and environment have been underway in the GATT for over two years. Considerable progress has been made in clarifying the issues and identifying some of their implications. Taking account of those discussions, an expanded programme of work was agreed to at the April 1994 Ministerial Conference held in Marrakesh to conclude the Uruguay Round trade negotiations. A new Trade and Environment Committee also was established at Marrakesh to pursue the expanded work programme. The Committee will report to the first Ministerial Conference following WTO implementation, at which time the work programme and status of the Committee will be reviewed.

Although no conclusions have been reached about the merit of proposals for change to the GATT/WTO and whether the process should at some point lead to a negotiating phase, a number of themes have emerged in the GATT discussions so far. Three points of consensus are worth mentioning at the outset.

First, there is no question about the importance of working towards improved environmental protection. All governments participating in the GATT discussions, which, of course, are the same governments meeting in other fora to address environmental issues, accept as a given the need to deal appropriately with these issues. It is clear, then, that the debate is not about environmental ends—it is about the means to those ends. It is about the *means* for action at the national and international levels, the means for international decision making and, specifically, what role the use of trade restrictions and the WTO should or should not play.

Second, it is widely agreed that there is already broad scope for using trade measures for environmental purposes under the existing GATT rules and that there exist confusion and misinformation on that score that are creating unnecessary concern. Governments have recognized that efforts should be made to clarify and better explain the relevant provisions and that this should be an important aspect of the work of the Trade and Environment Committee.

Third, all but the United States and Austria have rejected the unilateral use of trade restrictions as a means of imposing an environnmental programme on others.

Against this background, this Paper is intended to contribute to the on-going debate on the trade and environment question by providing an analysis of the main issues arising from proposals for change to the GATT/WTO and the key factors that will affect the process we will be engaged in over the next few years. On this basis, some objectives for Canada will be suggested, along with possible options for change to meet those objectives.

It should be noted that this Paper focuses on the proposals to loosen the trade rules for environmental purposes that have driven the debate so far. The Paper also identifies, however, emerging concerns in the business community in many countries about the trade distorting effects of certain environmental measures increasingly in use at the national level. The key issues and possible need for improved disciplines on some of these measures are flagged, but more detailed analysis remains to be done. Further work is planned to address this dimension of the trade and environment debate in greater depth.

ISSUES AND FACTORS

TO SET THE CONTEXT, IT IS USEFUL TO BEGIN with an indication of the scope under current GATT rules for using trade restrictions for environmental purposes and the nature of the proposals for change.

Current Scope for Using Trade Measures

As mentioned above, and contrary to a widespread perception among environmental groups, there is in fact broad scope in the GATT for using trade measures in support of environmental policies, programmes and standards. Essentially, the GATT provides under Article III, Article XX and elsewhere for the use of any type of trade restriction, including import and export quotas and prohibitions, or the imposition of taxes or other charges at the border, for the purpose of environmental protection or resource conservation within a country's jurisdiction, as long as basic requirements relating to non-discrimination and least-trade-restrictiveness are met (exceptions to the non-discrimination requirements are also possible). Of course, GATT/WTO member countries also could agree to the use of measures inconsistent with the trade rules amongst themselves in the context of a multilateral environmental programme.

Also contrary to the concerns of some, the GATT, and in particular the Technical Barriers to Trade (TBT) and Sanitary and Phytosanitary (SPS) Agreements, do not limit the ability of national governments to establish domestic standards of health and environmental protection and do not exert downward pressure on such standards. If based on international standards, there is a presumption that related trade measures taken at the national level do not conflict with the obligations in those Agreements. Standards higher than international norms also do not risk successful challenge, if they have a scientific basis (required under the SPS Agreement only) and are not more trade restrictive than necessary. This latter criterion seems to cause particular concern for some environmental groups, perhaps unnecessarily. The least-trade-restrictive requirement does not impose constraints on governments in setting the level of protection they consider appropriate; it simply indicates that trade should be disrupted as little as possible in the implementation of any related trade measures. It is not clear why this should be considered an unreasonable condition. Indeed, it is difficult to understand why it should be permissable to apply measures that are *more* trade restrictive than necessary.

In any event, there is no evidence that the requirements of the TBT and SPS Agreements present practical impediments to environmental protection. *Some 360 environment-related measures were notified under the TBT Agreement between 1980 and 1993, with not one being challenged.* The same can be said more generally of other GATT provisions. There has not been one single case where a trade restriction taken for legitimate environmental purposes has been successfully challenged in the GATT. The few cases usually cited as involving "environmental" issues, including the U.S.-Mexico "tuna-dolphin" case, reveal clear protectionist features upon closer examination.

Yet many environmentalists nevertheless express concern that the GATT and the WTO do not adequately address environmental issues or are even "anti-environment". When looked at more closely, however, it emerges that those claims all relate to one area of action that is indeed not authorized under the current rules: the use of trade penalties to press an environmental agenda extraterritorially. The objective is to use trade restrictions as a means to apply environmental or conservation standards outside a country's jurisdiction, including with respect to foreign process or production methods (PPMs), or to force participation in international environmental agreements (IEAs). It is true to say that the GATT does *not* provide for these types of measures.

This should not be considered surprising or an "oversight" in GATT negotiations, as is sometimes suggested. The fundamental *raison d'être* of the GATT has always been to discourage and ideally remove trade restrictions and to work to ensure that the international trading system is non-discriminatory, impartial and predictable. Successive rounds of multilateral trade negotiations have been aimed primarily at bringing down trade barriers and establishing rules to prevent the erection of new barriers to replace the old. In addition, the use of discriminatory or extraterritorial trade restrictions as a political tool to pursue other policy agendas has never been an objective of the multilateral trading rules. Indeed, there has been a long-standing consensus that the GATT should not serve as a forum for such political decision-making. This is reflected in the special exception provided under Article XXI, which clearly leaves political decisions on the use of trade sanctions to the United Nations, while ensuring that the GATT rules will not interfere when such decisions are taken. Proposals to introduce this type of political decision making into the GATT/WTO are, therefore, controversial, especially given their potential to create loopholes in the trade rules for a new generation of non-tariff protectionist measures that could quickly undermine the improved disciplines negotiated in the Uruguay Round.

There is in fact growing concern in the business community that there is already too much scope for the use of trade restrictions for environmental purposes. In particular, the GATT does not always provide clear and comprehensive disciplines with respect to trade-related environmental measures, such as eco-labelling, packaging, recycling and disposal requirements, eco-taxes and other types of economic instruments. It is becoming increasingly apparent that the use of such measures at the national level, often with different approaches being taken from one country to another and often with extraterritorial and PPM-based measures involved, can lead to significant and perhaps unwarranted impacts on trade. For example, important Canadian exports in the forest products sector are already under threat as a result of the use or proposed use of such measures, particularly within the U.S. and EU. And there is often no environmental justification for applying these measures to imports.

Proposals for Change and Implications

The Environmental Agenda

The pressure for change has so far come mainly from environmental NGOs. The basic agenda for many NGOs and some developed countries, particularly the U.S., is in fact to obtain authority in the GATT for the use of the types of trade restrictions or sanctions mentioned above. Although proposals to date have not provided much detail, they basically call for authorization of:

- the use of trade restrictions to apply environmental and conservation standards *extraterritorially*, i.e., with respect to matters under the jurisdiction of another country or in the global commons (as in Austria's attempt to regulate forest management practices in tropical timber producing countries and the U.S. tuna/dolphin case);
- the use of trade restrictions on goods based on concerns about the environmental effects of the foreign *PPM* (also an element in the tropical timber and tuna/dolphin cases, as well as potentially in the Montreal Protocol on Ozone Depleting Substances);
- the imposition of duties on imported goods to "adjust" for differences in environmental standards or enforcement in

other countries or to "internalize" costs, i.e., so-called *"eco-dumping"* or *"green countervail"* (as it is an alleged failure of government to require the full assumption of environmental costs that is at issue here, the term "green countervail" will be used in this Paper); and
- the use of *discriminatory trade restrictions or sanctions* to force participation in IEAs (e.g., the Montreal Protocol).

In addition, environmental NGOs seek direct participation in GATT/WTO proceedings as a central element of their agenda.

The proposals of most NGOs and the U.S. include *unilateral* use of the above types of trade restrictions. Other governments active in the GATT discussions, including Canada, have focused on *multilateral* approaches. The implications of unilateralism as opposed to the multilateral approach are, in fact, central to the trade and environment debate and need to be considered in some detail. The key issues regarding unilateralism are on what basis a country could seek to impose its standards on others and the implications of endorsing this approach. For Canada, there are important NAFTA overtones, given our rejection of the use of trade sanctions in the trilateral environmental side agreement as a tool for ensuring the enforcement of each country's domestic standards (let alone to empower one NAFTA Party to extend its standards to others). On the multilateral approach, it will be seen that, to the extent trade restrictions are needed at all, much can be done through the use of GATT-consistent measures. Furthermore, even the two types of GATT-inconsistent measures most at issue—PPMs and trade sanctions against non-parties to IEAs—might be acceptable if there were international consensus on their use.

a) Unilateralism Versus the Multilateral Approach

Proposals for the *unilateral* use of the types of trade restrictions identified above raise two key issues. First, what would be the justification for one country to use trade penalties to impose its standards on others whose circumstances, including environmental endowments, scientific assessments, environmental priorities, capacities to address competing objectives, societal values and so on, might legitimately lead to a different approach? In fact, what might be appropriate for one country will not necessarily be appropriate or viable for another, a fundamental point that was agreed at UNCED and has been endorsed by all except the U.S. in the GATT discussions.

In the case of PPMs and "green countervail," a concern about competitiveness is sometimes offered as the rationale. It is argued that industries in countries with higher or more consistently enforced environmental standards face an unfair competitive disadvantage against those in countries with lower or less strictly enforced standards and that imposing a charge on imports is justified to "equalize" the resulting differences in production costs. The need to ensure cost "internalization" is a related, although separate argument that is also often made.

The competitiveness issue raises a number of significant questions. To begin with, there is very little evidence that the costs associated with higher environmental standards (estimated to average only 1-2% of total production costs in most sectors) are significant enough when compared to other cost elements to be singled out as *the* factor critically affecting competitiveness. The GATT does not, in fact, provide for adjusting other types of cost differences at the border, such as those relating to labour, health or safety standards, other social programmes, energy costs, tax regimes and so on, most if not all of which are likely more significant factors than environmental standards. Why, then, should environmental standards be treated differently from a competitiveness perspective and what would the implications be of setting a precedent in this area (note in particular the views of the U.S. and some members of the EU regarding the need to "adjust" for differences in labour standards, social programmes and so on)?

And how would such trade measures be designed and administered? How would comparisons between different countries' standards, enforcement, production methods and their environmental impacts and costs be performed and by whom? How could such measures, particularly on PPMs which often cannot be detected in a finished product, be administered at the border? This difficulty has been recognized in a recent review by parties to the Montreal Protocol of the provision in the Protocol requiring consideration of the use of PPM-based import restrictions. It was concluded that, among other things, it would not, in fact, be feasible to administer such measures even though only a few countries would have been targets. The feasibility problem would be even more pronounced if imports from many countries were involved.

At the same time, measures that would penalize failures to enforce standards could have the environmentally counterproductive effect of dissuading countries from trying to raise those standards progressively (which they might not always be able to enforce fully).

Similar sorts of difficulties arise with the notion of regulating cost internalization through the trade rules. Of course, the key problem is that agreement would first be required on what the costs are and modalities for their fair and equitable reflection in the prices of goods, something that would probably need to be done on a sector-by-sector basis. Failing agreement on the underlying cost calculations, it is difficult to see how agreement could be reached in the GATT/WTO on the use of the trade rules as an enforcement mechanism. Moreover, the focus on current standards is somewhat misleading. If the principle of cost internalization were applied properly as part of the overall equation, countries that might otherwise push this approach would be exposed (e.g., water costing in California agriculture, energy consumption/emissions in the North, etc.). It is fair to enquire whether those countries pushing the environmental standards agenda are prepared to address such matters.

A second key issue regarding unilateralism is that the unilateral denial of market access is a tool that can only be used to any consistent effect by large countries, indeed probably only by the U.S. and EU. If unilateral actions were authorized, economic might would be used more easily and frequently to dictate the environmental policies and programmes of other countries. Moreover, the design and implementation of such measures would be based on unilateral judgements about the circumstances in other countries. It is clear that this approach would disadvantage smaller, export dependent countries not only in terms of their trade interests but also with regard to their ability to decide domestic environmental policy and priorities.

All these factors argue strongly that the unilateral approach is not in Canada's interest. Although there might be some scope for using access to our market to apply pressure on some smaller countries, Canada does not have a large enough market to employ this tactic in any consistent or meaningful way. Certainly, Canada is not in a position to impose standards or resource conservation programmes on our major trading partners, most notably the U.S. and EU.

At the same time, however, we easily could find ourselves on the receiving end, with the added danger that protectionist objectives might underlie stated environmental purposes. Indeed, there is a clear need to guard against the hijacking of environmental purposes by protectionists. As Sir Leon Brittan of the Eurpean Commission has warned, there is a serious risk of protectionist interests donning the "fashionable cloak of environmentalism". For example, as the U.S. exhausts the traditional countervailing duty procedure as a means of imposing restrictions on Canadian softwood lumber exports, it is not difficult to imagine what could be done if authority existed to impose levies unilaterally at the border to "adjust" for alleged differences in environmental standards or programmes. As mentioned, it was made clear in the NAFTA context that Canada would not wish to be subject to trade penalties by the U.S., even in the case of findings that our *own* standards are not being fully enforced.[1] This position is even more valid in a GATT context, particularly since the proposals being made are aimed at allowing the imposition of *another country's* standards. We cannot risk losing what we preserved in NAFTA through changes in the GATT.

Of course, the above points do not mean that unilateral measures will never be used. The U.S., EU and others have already taken such actions and undoubtedly will do so again if the circumstances, including political, suggest it. There always will be some degree of exposure for Canada. There may even be cases (e.g., in the fisheries area) in which the Canadian government also will be under pressure to take unilateral steps. The issue, however, is not whether unilateral action will ever be taken, but whether to provide authority in the GATT/WTO to allow for, and thus encourage, this approach. *The bottom line is that this would lead to a weakening of the law of the rules-based trading system we have worked hard to develop in favour of the law of the jungle. On balance, this is clearly not in Canada's interest,* either from a trade or an environmental point of view.

It has been widely agreed internationally (e.g., at UNCED, in the OECD and in the GATT discussions to date) that trade restrictions, even if used on a multilateral basis, are not the best or most appropriate means to achieve environmental objectives. Measures that deal directly with the root cause of the environmental problem and incentives that enable countries to cooperate, such as financial and technical assistance, will be more effective and efficient. There are, nevertheless, instances in which trade measures are used or may be proposed, either to accompany measures to control production, use or disposal of environmentally hazardous goods or for other reasons.

If use of the market access tool is considered on a *multilateral* basis, the issues that arise are somewhat different from those discussed above regarding the unilateral approach. To begin with, the issue of *justification* is minimized. To the extent that there is international consensus on an environmental programme or standard, there is no longer a question of one country or a group of countries imposing a solution on others—a common programme or standard will have been adopted by the international community. If the programme is properly developed, the problems identified above relating to extraterritoriality, PPMs, competitiveness concerns and administrative arbitrariness disappear or become much less pronounced. In addition, the effectiveness of a majority of countries acting together clearly will be greater than that of one or a small number acting alone. There can be no doubt that the multilateral approach is the way to go.

The main issue that then arises is what can be done if one or a few countries not cooperating in the programme threaten to undermine the effort being made by the international community, the concern often voiced by environmental NGOs. Although there may be a valid point here, the problems are perhaps not as unmanageable as sometimes feared. Even a brief examination of the dynamics of a well-designed multilateral programme negotiated through an IEA helps to put the issue into perspective.

First, if it is decided that trade measures will be used amongst participating countries as part of the environmental programme (which could be the case when controls on internationally traded goods or substances are involved), there is considerable scope to extend those measures to non-participating countries in a *GATT-consistent* manner, i.e., controlling or banning imports or exports from *all* sources on a national treatment, MFN basis. If the majority of countries applied trade restrictions in this way, the effect would be to constrain or eliminate world markets for participants and non-participants alike. In other words, if most of the countries involved in the production or consumption of a traded good or substance decided to control or eliminate their production and consumption, non-participants would face the disappearance of any meaningful sources of supply or export markets.[2]

To be most effective, of course, it would be necessary to have clear, enforceable commitments amongst parties to the IEA. Most existing IEAs are inadequate in this regard. The extent to which non-parties could continue environmentally hazardous activities or resist conservation efforts would be increased by a lack of clear obligations on, and compliance by, parties. In addition, the justification for and utility of imposing on non-parties requirements that are not being met by parties would be in question.[3]

If an IEA meets these basic tests, however, much can be done in a non-discriminatory, GATT-consistent way to use trade measures to extend the environmental programme to a minority of non-parties. In fact, as has emerged in the GATT discussions so far, there would appear to be only two types of trade measures that have been used or proposed for use that would not be GATT-consistent: restrictions on products from non-parties based on environmental concerns about the *PPM* as opposed to the product itself; and *discriminatory* trade restrictions against non-parties intended to pressure them to accept the environmental programme. Other types of GATT-inconsistent measures may be identified as work continues, but none has emerged so far.

The use of *PPM* measures might be proposed in a case where continued activities by a small number of non-participants could compromise the efforts being made by the rest of the international community to deal with a global environmental problem. Trade sanctions also might be proposed in such cases, particularly where trade restrictions on a national treatment and MFN basis would not be effective in addressing a problem with a non-participant. For example, restrictions on the environmentally damaging goods can effectively extend controls to non-participants only if they are in fact trading in those goods. If their production and consumption are entirely domestic, trade restrictions could only be applied to *other* products, as sanctions to force acceptance of the IEA.

The main questions that then arise regarding the use of PPM measures and trade sanctions are whether they are *necessary* and likely to be *effective,* and whether they are *justified.* Necessity and effectiveness can only be judged on a case-by-case basis depending on the circumstances involved. The same would be true on the issue of justification. In the type of scenarios just identified, however, *an argument could be made that the presence of international consensus would provide grounds for the use of both PPM measures and trade sanctions by the international community against hold-out countries.* The issue then becomes how to establish what constitutes an international consensus. We return to this question below.

Before moving on, though, a few points about the types of situations that could arise would be useful to keep the discussion in perspective. In particular, a word about so-called "free riders" is in order. Although this term is often used, it has never been clearly defined.

It is, perhaps, easiest to start with what it generally would *not* mean. It presumably would not be used to describe countries that for objective reasons do not accept the science and risk assessment behind, or the objectives or provisions of, the environmental agreement in question. It is a recognized complexity of dealing with environmental problems that the science can take time to develop and may not always be definitive, resulting in the possibility of legitimate differences of view as to the extent and implications of the problem and the most balanced and effective way to deal with it. The likelihood that such disagreements can and will occur underlines the importance of seeking broad international consensus on new environmental disciplines.

Similarly, we should not describe countries that have different environmental priorities as free riders if they elected or were forced by more limited means to concentrate their resources in other areas of environmental protection. All countries have to make choices in their pursuit of improved environmental protection and their choices may not always be the same. Governments may wish to try to persuade other countries to accept their own priorities and even offer assistance to this end. But we should be cautious about condemning as free riders those who have other serious environmental problems that they consider more pressing or who simply cannot absorb the costs of adaptation or enforcement.

So, what is really meant by "free rider"? The U.S. suggested early on in the GATT discussions that free riders are those who decline to assume the obligations of an environmental agreement in order to avoid the costs that might be involved while still benefitting from the environmental improvements being made by others. This perspective involves the notion of non-parties obtaining commercial, competitive advantage over other countries. But how and by whom would judgements be made about the motivations of countries reluctant to participate? On what basis would it be determined that there might be economic, commercial interests involved when other reasons for not participating were identified?

And what about situations in which the economic concerns of a country, whether developed or developing, constitute a practical or political impediment preventing that country from pursuing an environmental programme more aggressively? No government is immune from this type of reality. For example, the U.S. itself (the main proponent of the use of trade restrictions to force other countries to accept its preferred environmental programmes, standards or agreements) actively opposed the establishment of meaningful targets for the reduction of greenhouse gases under the Climate Change Convention for openly stated economic reasons. It also initially refused to sign the Biodiversity Convention and has now attached its own caveats in order to assert its intention to protect strictly its domestic industry's intellectual property rights. The former head of the U.S. Environmental Protection Agency, James Reilly, stated publicly that the U.S. would not accept any environmental agreement that would adversely affect the U.S. economy. In areas where it might be out of step with the international community or the country most responsible for slowing down the pace, would the U.S. be prepared to be on the receiving end of trade restrictions aimed at forcing it to agree to programmes being advanced by others?

Perhaps the term free rider is something of a misnomer in relation to environmental agreements. It seems more appropriate to think in terms of non-parties whose actions could undermine the efforts being made by parties to tackle a global problem and what steps could be taken in this type of situation. As mentioned, a range of positive measures, including financial and technological assistance, should be considered first. In certain circumstances, especially if other options have been exhausted, the international community also might decide to employ trade restrictions or sanctions to force compliance by the hold-out country. It seems unlikely, however, that this would be a frequent event. Certainly there should be no doubt that it would be a complex and difficult situation to address. At the end of the day, the discussion always points back to the critical issue of how to identify whether an international consensus exists that might justify the use of punitive measures against non-parties. We return to this point below.

b) NGO Access to the GATT

Another important element in the environmental NGO agenda is to seek institutional changes that would allow them to participate directly in GATT/WTO consultations, negotiations and dispute settlement proceedings. These proposals were considered in the Uruguay Round. On dispute settlement, clearer provision has been made for the release of non-confidential versions of panel submissions and the possibility of panels requesting information from relevant experts. However, proposals for direct participation by NGOs were not accepted. They can be expected to continue to press their demands. The stated NGO view is that environmental considerations must be taken into account and generally should prevail over trade considerations in the development and implementation of the trade rules.

Part of the environmental community's concern arises from the view that the GATT has been a "closed shop," making it difficult to know how the system works and how issues are being dealt with. Traditionally, there in fact has been little attention paid to the GATT except by industries whose interests are directly affected by, for example, tariff or other negotiations that establish the terms of market access (it is important to note that even those groups with a longstanding stake do not have direct access—they pursue their concerns at the national level). The GATT, therefore, has not been accustomed to demands for direct involvement by private interests. There also are real constraints on the extent to which NGOs in any field can participate, not the least of which is that only governments have responsibility and accountability for negotiating on behalf of all their national interests. Other critical mandate considerations are discussed further below.

While there are certain clear limitations, there is also a need to respond to the "closed shop" concern, recognizing the appropriate roles and responsibilities of governments, NGOs and the GATT/WTO itself. It is in everyone's interest to provide for a good exchange of information and better transparency on how the system works, what the rules are, what the appropriate interface with other policy areas is, and so on. It also will be important to bring together the full range of interested parties—business and labour groups, development NGOs, and a range of UN Agencies, to name just a few. This would allow for a direct exchange of views amongst all interested parties.

A number of possible consultative mechanisms could be considered. For example, the GATT Secretariat has already met on several occasions with NGOs and business groups and will be using more comprehensive symposia to bring together a wide range of interests. This type of mechanism could be continued on a regular basis. The key would be to focus the process on issues appropriate to the GATT's role and mandate and to ensure openness to all interested participants.

The proposals that call for direct participation of environmental NGOs in GATT/WTO consultations, negotiations and dispute settlement cases, however, raise fundamental questions about the role, mandate and functioning of the trade organization. There is considerable confusion and contradiction in the trade and environment debate in this regard. On one hand, the environmental community believes strongly that the GATT should not make judgements about nor interfere with the environmental policies and priorities of member countries. This view is entirely valid and has been endorsed by governments in the GATT discussions. At the same time, however, the objective of NGOs in seeking to participate directly is in fact to introduce environmental policy arguments in what is envisaged as a process of weighing environmental values against trade values in GATT negotiations and dispute settlement cases. This is what some NGOs believe should have occurred in the panels on the U.S. tuna/dolphin measures, the case that in fact gave rise to the proposals for institutional change. The view is that NGOs should have been able to participate directly in the panel in order to present the argument that the objective of protecting dolphins should prevail over the GATT rights of Mexico and others.

The problem is that this approach would indeed cast a panel and the GATT/WTO more generally in the role of making judgements about the relative merits of members' environmental policies and practices. Unless a blank cheque approach were adopted in which *any* stated environmental objective would automatically override GATT rights (which may be what some NGOs have in mind, but which clearly would open the door to abuse and therefore would be unacceptable), cases could arise in which a panel decided that the environmental objective involved should *not* prevail over GATT rights. Or a panel could find itself having to arbitrate between the environmental policies of two or more governments. This result would run counter to the other stated NGO view that the GATT must not judge nor interfere with any country's environmental policies or priorities.

The proponents of this approach will have to recognize that they cannot have it both ways. The bottom line is that the GATT/WTO is not an environmental organization, has no mandate or competence to judge or make environmental policy and, therefore, should not be used as a forum for debate on environmental policy issues.

The other factor is that direct participation by environmental NGOs would open the door to participation by many other lobbyists: business groups, labour unions, development NGOs, consumer groups and so on. The practical effect of this would be to create a two-tier system—one process allowing participation by a variety of non-governmental groups and a second private process for actual government-to-government negotiations or panel deliberations. The basic nature of the system would not change, it simply would become less efficient and considerably more time consuming.

The appropriate channel for consultation with interest groups is at the national level in the preparation of government positions.[4] It is governments that are the accountable and, in most cases, the democratically elected representatives of *all* domestic interests, not just of one set of non-governmental players.

A balance, therefore, needs to be struck—more openness and better exchange of information will be important, but the line must be drawn at direct participation in GATT/WTO consultations, negotiations and dispute settlement proceedings for both mandate and process reasons. This approach is comparable to the arrangements that are in place in other fora, including the OECD and UN.

The Trading Agenda

The preceding section sets out the environmental agenda, which was the source and so far has been the focus of the trade and environment debate. Although less active to date than the environmental NGOs, the business community in many countries, both developed and developing, is beginning to express increasing concern about the adverse trade impacts of environmental measures used at the national level, such as those mentioned earlier relating to "environmentally friendly" packaging and disposal requirements, eco-labelling, eco-taxes and other types of economic instruments. Proposals for a tightening of GATT disciplines in this regard can be expected.

Although more dimensions may emerge as work in this area progresses, two basic issues have been a focus of attention so far. First, there is the case in which the environmental objectives underlying the measure may be valid and very similar, but countries are adopting widely different approaches for pursuing those objectives. This results in a situation in which exporters must adapt their products to a growing variety of conflicting requirements in order to maintain access to foreign markets. Of course, it usually is the case that national authorities take closer account of the circumstances and needs of domestic producers than those of foreign competitors, which builds a bias against imports into most systems. The resulting situation can impose a burden on exporters that is arguably unjustifiable and also avoidable through international cooperation and coordination. There also is, once again, the clear need to guard against protectionist abuse. This is a serious potential problem with any use of trade restrictions for environmental purposes, but is perhaps particularly relevant to these types of national measures. The development of international programmes and standards or mutual recognition schemes in the appropriate fora (e.g., the International Standards Association (ISO), the Food and Agriculture Organization (FAO), the International Tropical Timber Organization (ITTO), through bilateral or plurilateral consultations, etc.) and the inclusion of related disciplines in the GATT/WTO will need to be examined.

Second, there are a number of situations in which the environmental justification for applying certain requirements to imported goods is questionable. For example, should PPM criteria aimed at addressing a purely local environmental objective be applied equally to imported products from countries where that objective is either not relevant or where there is no basis for the importing country to dictate a standard? This issue has already arisen for Canada with respect to the application to Canadian exports of requirements in the U.S. for recycled content in paper products and various criteria for eco-labels and eco-taxes in the EU. The potential for other such situations is great. It would be helpful to undertake more detailed studies of areas where Canadian exports could be particularly vulnerable to these types of measures, especially in the U.S. and EU. At the same time, we will need to have detailed information on what is being done in Canada, including at the provincial and industry levels.

For all the above types of measures, the need to provide clear environmental justification for the application of domestic requirements to imports, the issues of PPMs and extraterritoriality, and the relevance of the national treatment principle will have to be addressed.

Another important issue that is central to the work in GATT is whether there is adequate provision for notification of and consultation on such measures, or what is referred to as transparency. It is widely recognized that there are problems of compliance with existing requirements and gaps in transparency provisions for certain types of measures. It will be necessary to identify all such gaps and then consider what changes might be appropriate to close them and work toward improved compliance.

a) Negotiability

A critical factor in developing the Canadian position on all the above issues and proposals is an assessment of their negotiability, not only "the art of the possible," but how they fit into wider foreign policy issues. Although the GATT process is still in an analytical phase, with no agreement on whether or when a prescriptive phase might be engaged, it is already possible to identify some basic negotiability factors. In particular, the general approach and agenda of developing countries is already quite clear (although the most active and prominent developing countries in the process so far have been India, Brazil, Mexico and the ASEAN countries, their views appear to be broadly representative of other developing countries and the economies in transition as well). The concerns and objectives of this group of players will have to be reflected before any negotiation, as demanded by some developed countries, could begin.

In many respects, the concerns and objectives of developing and smaller developed countries are the same. With respect to the environmental agenda described above as well as the growing concern about the impact on exports of various types of environmental measures at the national level, the issues do not fall along North/South lines, but rather reflect a big/small split. Beyond these issues, however, there are a number of points unique to the developing country agenda, such as transfer of technology, special market access, the need for financial transfers and so on. As will be seen, many of these developing country interests will be difficult to meet, which in turn will limit what some developed countries can expect to obtain.

Developing Countries

First and foremost, developing countries, along with many developed countries, are highly suspicious of the protectionist potential just beneath the surface of proposals to loosen GATT disciplines for stated environmental purposes. At the same time, they are alarmed and offended by the environmental agenda of using trade restrictions or sanctions to force acceptance of environmental programmes and standards. They are well aware that they would be the most vulnerable targets of such sanctions, and they reject their use on both trade and environmental grounds. They argue that trade penalties would actually interfere with their ability to address environmental problems by disrupting the economic development necessary to give them the means to pursue better environmental protection. Moreover, they see the preoccupation with the use of trade restrictions as further evidence of the limited willingness of developed countries to provide positive assistance to help developing countries respond to the North's environmental priorities. The perception is that instead of being offered carrots, developing countries are being asked under the GATT to arm developed countries with the sticks.

We need to recognize that these developing country concerns are valid and unlikely to change. Essentially, any proposal or formula that could provide GATT cover for the use of trade restrictions and sanctions by the economically strong against the economically weak or open the door for new variations on the protectionist theme will be fundamentally non-negotiable. This is true for both the *unilateral* use of such measures, including those described earlier with respect to PPMs and "green countervail," as well as for IEAs that provide for sanctions to force participation or the application of PPM-based restrictions, but do not meet a substantial threshold of broadly-based multilateral membership or support.

Having said this, developing countries *may* be prepared to consider ways to establish more clearly that the GATT rules should not impede the use of such measures in IEAs that *do* reflect the will of the international community. The threshold for recognizing broadly-based agreements obviously does not have to include all potentially concerned countries. To be negotiable, however, any formula for addressing IEAs could not be skewed against developing countries (as several proposed to date are). Canada also would do well to seek a substantial threshold.

In addition, developed countries will have to come to grips with the developing country agenda, a factor that has received little attention to date but will emerge more strongly in the post-Uruguay Round process. An important developing country objective will be to obtain improved disciplines on the use of environmental measures of the eco-labelling and packaging type identified above. There has been strong consensus in the GATT discussions so far that there are in fact problems in this area that need to be addressed. Indeed, while a key element in the developing country agenda, this is by no means only a developing country concern. Canadian interests are very similar on this issue and others as well. Proposals for tight controls on such measures can be expected, but it remains to be seen how far the U.S. and EU in particular, who presumably will face resistance from their domestic environmental NGOs, will be prepared to go.

Developing countries also will insist on resolving the long-outstanding issue of trade in domestically prohibited goods. An earlier GATT Working Party prepared a decision calling for the use of a Prior Informed Consent (PIC) system with respect to exports of domestically prohibited goods so that governments, particularly in developing countries, would have the opportunity to control or refuse proposed shipments of such goods. The issue is the use of developing countries as "dumping grounds" for trade in hazardous goods no longer permitted for sale in the developed country of origin.[5] The decision was blocked by the U.S., however, in light of opposition from domestic industries that do not wish to risk losing developing country export markets. Any continued U.S. resistance to resolving this issue will not only be a practical stumbling block to engaging developing countries, but also will be held up as an example of the hypocrisy that developing countries see in much of the trade and environment debate (e.g., developed countries advocate the use of trade restrictions to advance the environmental agenda, except in cases where their own economic interests could be affected).

Finally, developing countries will use the GATT process to press for further action to address their economic development goals through improved market access and technology transfer. The protection of intellectual property rights in the new Uruguay Round TRIPS Agreement will be brought into the picture (e.g., developing countries may seek agreed interpretations of TRIPS to allow compulsory licensing of technologies that would help meet the objective of environmentally sound development and also may pursue concerns about the ownership of and benefits from biological resources). Since the post-Uruguay Round work programme will include the development and technology transfer issues in the mainstream debate, developed countries will have to respond. However, there will be little, if anything, that can be offered on these fronts. Following the long and bruising Uruguay Round negotiations, the prospects for making more market access concessions or weakening the protection just agreed in TRIPS (where the U.S. and EU were the main demandeurs) are remote. As mentioned, an unwillingness to respond on these issues will further constrain what certain developed countries will be able to obtain on their agenda.

The U.S. and EU

In terms of the other key players, both the U.S. and EU have so far been driven primarily by concerns about responding to their environmental lobbies. The U.S. would appear to have the most ambitious objectives, although there have been conflicts within the Administration and no clear position has emerged. The main focus, however, seems to be on finding cover for trade restrictions to extend U.S. standards to others on both a unilateral and multilateral basis. The U.S. is isolated on the question of unilateralism and eventually will have to face that fact. But, for the time being, all options seem to be on their agenda.

When forced to retreat on seeking authority for unilateral trade restrictions of the tuna-dolphin variety, the U.S. is likely to continue to pursue a unilateral agenda under the guise of multilateralism. For example, the U.S. may argue for authority to take measures (unilaterally) in connection with an IEA or perhaps a UN resolution, even though they do not contain agreed provisions for, or definitions of, such measures. Unilateralism under the guise of multilateralism will bear close watching.

The main EU focus so far has been on seeking what amounts to a "blank cheque" exemption from GATT rules for IEAs, including "regional agreements," and to seek accommodation for the use of PPM-based measures under such IEAs (the section below on options for accommodating IEAs describes the EU proposal). The EU has stated its opposition to unilateral actions and the use of trade sanctions to force participation in IEAs, although it supports the trade sanctions in the Montreal Protocol and often points to this Agreement as the type it wants to exempt from GATT rules. It also has opposed the "green countervail" concept. In its interest in accommodating vaguely defined IEAs and regional agreements in the GATT, we will need to watch for an effort to establish a basis for using import restrictions for the extraterritorial application of standards on PPMs agreed by the EU member states and perhaps some of their neighbours. European Commission officials indicate publicly that this is not their intention, but there are contradictions in certain specific cases and apparent differences of view between the member states (e.g., during the recent renegotiation of the International Tropical Timber Agreement, some member states, initially supported by the Commission, sought unsuccessfully to use the Agreement to gain cover for trade restrictions based on PPMs and taken on a "multilateral" basis, meaning by the EU alone).

The EU position is, therefore, not entirely clear and also may shift with respect to sanctions and other issues. Environmental NGO pressures are mounting and the U.S. will be working with the EU to develop a common approach. Either of these players alone has a proven ability to use political force against other countries when driven by domestic lobbies. If they team up, the pressures will be very significant.

Summary

As this overview suggests, common ground for developed and developing countries may be found on the issues of accommodating the use of otherwise GATT-inconsistent trade measures in IEAs that represent international consensus (if an appropriate formula can be found), improving disciplines on and transparency in the use of trade-related environmental measures at the national level, and resolving the question of domestically prohibited goods. If the process could focus on this balance of issues, we may be able to move to a prescriptive phase that would address interests on all sides. If there is an insistence on pursuing proposals for amendments to authorize unilateral/extraterritorial actions, including on PPMs and "green countervail" measures, and the use of sanctions in IEAs in the absence of international consensus, an indefinite standoff can be expected to develop.

PROPOSED OBJECTIVES FOR CANADA

OVERALL, CANADA HAS AN INTEREST IN MOVING the process forward in order to respond meaningfully to the valid concerns of the environmental community and others, to deal expeditiously with the misconceptions about the GATT/environment interface that are a continuing source of unnecessary conflict and to address the increasingly valid concerns of Canadian exporters whose positions in foreign markets are under threat. Since the least negotiable proposals are not in the Canadian interest in any event, we should consider efforts to focus the discussion on the common ground issues identified above, concentrating in particular on the accommodation of the multilateral approach and better cooperation in and disciplines on the use of trade-related environmental measures at the national level.

Against this background, appropriate objectives could comprise the following:

- **To encourage greater openness and exchanges of information on the trade rules and the interface between the GATT/WTO and other policy areas through the use of consultative mechanisms such as regular symposia.**
- There clearly is a need to respond to the "closed shop" concern, while at the same time recognizing the appropriate roles and responsibilities of governments, NGOs and the GATT/WTO itself. More openness and a better exchange of information is important, but, in my view, the line must be drawn at direct participation in GATT/WTO consultations, negotiations and dispute settlement proceedings for both mandate and process reasons.

- **To clarify the extent to which the GATT rules provide scope for the use of trade measures for environmental purposes.**
- The inaccurate perception in some quarters that the GATT constitutes a significant barrier to the pursuit of legitimate national and international environmental policies and programmes needs to be corrected. At the same time, there are valid questions about the interpretation of the rules that should be addressed to the extent possible (bearing in mind that only a panel can judge consistency with the rules in a specific case).
- In addition, what role the GATT can and should play regarding environmental matters requires clarification. The appropriate limits of the GATT mandate should be better explained, including with respect to how account would be taken of an environmental programme or standard in a dispute settlement case involving a trade measure used in connection with that programme or standard (i.e., not making

value judgements about the merits of the environmental programme, but taking it as a given and focusing instead on how the trade measure relates to it).

- **To promote analysis of the types of trade measures proposed for environmental purposes that would fall outside the scope of GATT/WTO authorities, with a focus on the necessity and effectiveness of using such measures.**
- This is the approach that has been taken so far by Canada and most other participants in the process. It is necessary to be clear on what is being proposed for accommodation in the GATT/WTO in order to establish the basis for negotiating an appropriate formula for change. It also will be important to have grounds for not acting on proposals that are undesirable and non-negotiable.

- **To contribute to making the case against changes to the GATT rules to allow for unilateral trade restrictions aimed at applying environmental standards to or forcing their adoption by other countries.**
- This includes the unilateral use of PPM-based measures and "green countervail" duties. Measures aimed at imposing one country's standards on others are unjustifiable, administratively unfeasible and would not be in Canada's trade or environmental interest.

- **In the case of the possible use of GATT-inconsistent trade measures on a multilateral basis, to ensure that the GATT rules do not interfere with a decision by the international community to include such measures in a broadly-based IEA.**
- The challenge is to find an approach geared to IEAs that represent international consensus and meet basic criteria in terms of the specificity of the obligations involved, the trade measures to be used and the dispute settlement system for ensuring compliance. Proposals to exempt GATT-inconsistent trade provisions, i.e., *discriminatory* restrictions or sanctions against non-parties or *PPM-based* measures, in

IEAs that do *not* meet a reasonable threshold of participation or support would be undesirable and non-negotiable.
- The otherwise GATT-inconsistent trade restrictions that could be accommodated would include PPM-based measures.

- **With respect to the use of trade-related environmental measures such as eco-labelling and packaging requirements, eco-taxes and so forth, to find a means to ensure that they do not lead to an unnecessary disruption of trade, including the negotiation of appropriate safeguards in the WTO.**
- Canadian exports risk being adversely affected by the use of such measures at the national level, although their justification is not always evident. It is in Canada's interest to join other countries, including developing ones, to minimize the trade effects of such measures through the development of common standards in appropriate fora such as the ISO, providing for consultation and cooperation in their implementation, establishing mutual recognition systems where appropriate and so on. Improved disciplines in the GATT based on such approaches need to be developed.
- We also should work towards agreement, which will need to be reflected in all the relevant WTO Agreements, that requirements and criteria relating to local environmental circumstances should not be applied extraterritorially through their imposition on imported products.

OPTIONS

THIS SECTION FOCUSES ON THE LAST TWO of the above objectives, since they are the ones that would require actual changes to the trade rules. The objective of clarifying how the existing rules apply is also an important task and should be pursued as an element in the on-going work of the Trade and Environment Committee. There would be a number of possibilities for confirming and conveying agreed clarifications or interpretations of existing provisions, including reports and/or decisions by the relevant bodies in the WTO system. Member countries could consider the options as work progresses.

The following are basic options for addressing the questions of how to make clearer provision for widely-supported IEAs and to provide for improved disciplines on certain trade-related environmental measures.

Accommodating IEAs, Including Those That Might Use PPM-based Measures

As background to any discussion of options for accommodating IEAs, it is necessary to flag a number of horizontal themes or considerations that have emerged in the GATT discussions, which generally reflect presentational or perceptual concerns that need to be resolved. In particular, there is a strong view in the environmental community that the GATT/WTO must not be seen to sit in judgement of the work of environmental negotiators or to be approving or rejecting IEAs. Although the environmental community acknowledges that IEAs should not have a "blank cheque" exemption from the trade rules, given the potential for abuse, many are uncomfortable with any possibility of what is seen as a GATT/WTO review of IEAs in a dispute settlement case or otherwise. Similarly, industry groups and trade experts are uncomfortable with the suggestion that IEAs should be allowed to breach GATT rules, which embody carefully balanced contractual rights, with no effective recourse against possible abuse.

Before any progress can be made, it will be necessary to get past such presentational sensitivities and, once again, place the role of the GATT/WTO into proper perspective. Clearly, the blank cheque approach is neither advisable nor negotiable. This means that there will need to be a channel for checking trade measures in IEAs against the trade rules to guard against abuse, while at the same time ensuring that the GATT could not be used to impede international consensus on an IEA in the same way that the GATT does not constitute a road block to, for example, the use of trade sanctions pursuant to a UN Security Council decision.

Three key points need to be made clear. First, under no circumstance should the *environmental* objectives or provisions of an IEA be judged in the GATT. The GATT rules would enter the picture only if trade measures actually taken pursuant to an IEA were challenged as a violation of a country's GATT rights *or* if parties to an IEA themselves wished to preclude such a challenge by seeking an exemption from *their* obligations. Either way, the GATT/WTO should not judge the environmental issue or programme involved, let alone approve or reject the IEA itself.

Second, there are legal realities governing the relationship between treaties that must be recognized. Over 100 governments have negotiated the trade rules over the years in pursuit of their national interests, acquiring rights and accepting obligations in the process. Parties to an IEA could decide to set aside their own GATT rights for the purpose of that IEA, but they would have no power under the IEA to set aside the GATT rights of others. Any limitation of non-parties' GATT rights could only be achieved under the GATT itself.

Third, the environmental community's concern that the GATT/WTO not be involved in or sit in judgement of an IEA underlines the importance of focusing on the accommodation of broadly-based IEAs representing international consensus. If exceptions from GATT obligations were sought in cases where such consensus had not been reached, the GATT could indeed be thrust into the debate or disagreement on the underlying environmental issue. This would be in no-one's interest.

Partly in light of the presentational questions, the discussion of possible options is sometimes expressed in terms of the relative advantages or disadvantages of a "positive testing"/"*ex-ante*" approach (obtaining exceptions for trade provisions in IEAs in advance) *versus* a "negative testing" / "*ex-post*" approach (defending measures that have been challenged). The various approaches are not mutually exclusive. Clarifying existing rules to the extent possible is relevant to both approaches. Providing exceptions to prevent challenges points towards positive testing/ex-ante solutions.

Against this background, there would appear to be three basic options for consideration:

- *clarifying/expanding* the application of the *existing criteria* of GATT Article XX to provide greater scope regarding the type of measures that could be used in IEAs and defended under that Article;
- providing a *general exception* for IEAs in Article XX, through either an agreed interpretation of the existing Article or an amendment to it; or
- providing for a *case-by-case exception or waiver* from GATT rules specially tailored to IEAs under Article XX or the new GATT/WTO waiver provisions.

The first two options are reflected in informal proposals already made in the GATT discussions by the Nordics and EU respectively. The relevance of the waiver approach also has been discussed in general terms, although based on the current provisions of GATT Article XXV which clearly are inadequate for this purpose. *Given the basic considerations that follow, in my view the best approach, and probably the most negotiable option, would be the specially-tailored case-by-case exception or waiver.* This does not mean to suggest that a negotiation will be easy to engage or that the outcome will be guaranteed. Amending the GATT/WTO is an ambitious undertaking, requiring broad agreement amongst a large number of participants with widely-varying interests and concerns. Nothing should be taken for granted. In particular, it must be recognized that developing countries likely will not be prepared to consider a negotiation until it is clear that their needs, including on increased disciplines on environmental measures, will be covered. Canada should take the same approach.

Clarifying/Expanding the Application of the Article XX Criteria to IEAs.

A clarification of the existing rules is already an objective in the process and could be helpful in providing guidance on the use of certain types of measures in IEAs, or even purely national measures. For instance, it may be possible to develop indicative examples of various types of GATT-inconsistent restrictions that could be covered by Article XX (e.g., in the case of standards relating to product characteristics where imports from countries meeting and certifying the standards would be allowed, while imports from countries not doing so would be prohibited—a discriminatory import ban).

It is difficult, however, to envisage a basis for agreeing on an *expanded* application of the existing criteria to allow for the types of trade restrictions that currently fall outside Article XX and are, therefore, the ones most at issue, i.e., trade sanctions against non-parties and PPMs. Essentially, this would involve addressing directly and in a "boiler plate" way the question of when trade restrictions could be used, indeed would be "necessary," to force participation in IEAs or apply PPM standards to countries that do not agree with them. A number of questions arise:

- How would criteria be defined in generally applicable terms to cover fully what likely would be widely-varying circumstances regarding future IEAs? How would the Article XX requirement that such measures not constitute "arbitrary or unjustifiable discrimination between countries where the same conditions prevail" be defined? What would "the same conditions" mean with respect to environmental matters where domestic circumstances and policies might be legitimately different? How could all these elements be defined to ensure relevance to any possible future IEA?
- For example, it has been suggested that "the same conditions" could be taken to prevail with respect to a non-party to an IEA *only* if that country had the same environmental policies or programmes as those required under the IEA. This would mean, however, that non-participation would, by definition, expose a non-party to trade discrimination, even if it had legitimate environmental or other policy reasons to differ on the approach to the environmental issue.

Proposing this approach as a general rule would not only be difficult to defend, it would, in my view, be non-negotiable.
- And how would the Article XX principle of least trade-restrictiveness be applied to the situation where the purpose is in fact to be intentionally trade restrictive in order to exert pressure on another country to force change in its domestic policies? In the context of the highly-charged issue of trade sanctions, there will be fundamentally different views on these questions. It is difficult to see a basis for reaching agreement on making the existing criteria fit.
- Moreover, it is not at all clear that the GATT/WTO is even the right place to address such questions. The use of trade sanctions is first and foremost a matter of international environmental policy making, i.e., what tools does the international community wish to have available to advance and enforce the environmental agenda and under what type of circumstances could those tools be used? If consensus on this question were reached in the appropriate environmental forum, means could be provided to recognize and not interfere with that consensus in the GATT/WTO. But it would be difficult for the GATT/WTO to establish criteria *a priori.*
- Indeed, developing countries in particular could be expected simply to reject any explicit accommodation of such measures in the trade rules in the absence of a consensus on the underlying environmental issues, generally or in the context of a specific IEA.

While this approach may be pursued by some participants, and we should be prepared to work on clarifying the existing criteria, it seems unlikely that a meaningful answer to the IEA issue could be found with this option.

Providing a General Exception for IEAs in Article XX

The EU has put this option on the table. The basic proposal is to reach agreement on an interpretation of the existing Article XX that would constitute a general exception for IEAs, thus precluding any challenge of GATT-inconsistent measures they might contain (the significant and sweeping nature of such a general exception would go beyond the scope of an interpretation of the rules—a formal amendment would need to be considered). The concept and justification are that, in the case of a broadly-based IEA representing true international consensus, the GATT/WTO should recognize that consensus and provide for the exemption of any trade restrictions judged necessary. The concept is sound as far as it goes, but a number of difficulties quickly emerge in considering how it could be captured properly with a general exception approach:

- The basic problem is how to define *generally* and for almost *automatic* application the type of IEA that would qualify for the exception, covering any possible future case, while protecting against abuse. In its proposal, the EU depends on a *process approach.* Any IEA would qualify as long as it were negotiated in an open process under the auspices of the UN with any country allowed to become a member. One major flaw, however, is that here there is nothing to test for *actual participation,* which would be the only real measure of the degree of international acceptance of the IEA. An IEA with limited membership, and significant opposition, would be covered under the EU proposal. Moreover, if only the process aspects are considered, other critical features (e.g., effective compliance provisions) would be overlooked. In fact, what the EU has suggested is *not* a general exception in practice, but rather a procedure with only one, very loose criterion to apply to all IEAs.
- In reality, it is, in fact, extremely difficult to define generally, once again in a "boiler plate" fashion, what threshold of participation would constitute international consensus for application to *all* IEAs. Circumstances will vary with each case. A so-called general exception would amount to a blank cheque, which is not only undesirable, but non-negotiable as well. The negative reaction in the GATT discussions to date to the substance of the EU proposal demonstrates this clearly. Indeed, if an attempt were made

to negotiate a threshold of participation in order to define what IEAs would be eligible for such a loose special exception, it is likely that many participants in that negotiation, recognizing that there might be IEAs they will not join in future, would set the bar for entry impossibly high.

A Case-by-Case Exception or Waiver[6]

As the above suggests, the best, and likely most negotiable, option would appear to be a case-by-case exception approach comprising several criteria. This could be devised under Article XX or as a "Special Environmental Waiver" under the WTO waiver provisions. In Article XX, an exception could be established for the trade provisions of specific IEAs listed in an Annex, along the lines of the NAFTA Article 104 provision. The inclusion of an IEA on the list would require approval through a voting procedure as used for waivers.

With respect to the waiver approach, it is clear that the existing provisions are not well suited to the IEA case (the limited duration of a waiver, the requirement for annual review and the presentational concern that the traditional waiver is viewed as relating to "exceptional" cases). To address these shortcomings, a procedure specifically tailored to the IEA case could be established. In either approach, the following elements would need to be included.

To qualify for the exception procedure, an IEA would have to meet a number of basic criteria:

- There would need to be a general indication that the request relates to a broadly-based international agreement. As mentioned, it is extremely difficult to define in any dependable and generally applicable way what constitutes a sufficient level of participation to denote consensus. Nevertheless, there would need to be a basic threshold for accessing the exception or waiver procedure, in order to avoid disputed IEAs or those with low levels of participation being brought forward. The net effect of seeking GATT/WTO authority to use PPMs or trade sanctions to force

acceptance of IEAs that do not enjoy broad support would be to push the underlying disagreement on the environmental issue into another forum which has neither the mandate nor the expertise to deal with it. The GATT/WTO should not interfere with IEAs representing international consensus on an environmental issue, but it cannot be cast in the role of referee when the issue or IEA is in dispute.
- The basic threshold could be indicated by reference to level of participation, particularly by a substantial majority of countries affected (including users of the goods or substance in question). Developing countries also would insist on reference to participation by countries having different levels of development and geographical location. The basic threshold along these lines (other elements could be proposed) would be *indicative* that a specific IEA is in the right "ball park," but would not be *definitive* regarding all future cases. The subsequent test of consensus or vote on the exception or waiver request would be the check in any particular case. The actual level of participation in a specific case could vary depending on the circumstances involved. This avoids the problem with the general exception approach of having to set a very high, general threshold in order to prevent abuse.
- The IEA would have to contain clear and enforceable obligations for parties. This would include an effective compliance/dispute settlement system. It would not be reasonable to seek to waive the GATT/WTO rights of non-parties in order to enforce an IEA against them (or to confirm, for greater certainty, the waiving of GATT/WTO rights of *parties* to an IEA), if parties were not prepared to enforce the IEA amongst themselves, under effective terms established in the IEA itself.
- The trade provisions in the IEA also would need to be set out clearly, including with respect to measures to be taken at the national level. In the absence of a reasonable indication of the trade measures involved (e.g., how and when they might apply), it would not be possible to know what was being accommodated.

- In terms of timing, as the above points suggest, the procedure would need to triggered after the development of the substantive provisions of the IEA, but before any challenge of trade measures taken at the national level. It would, therefore, be an *ex-ante* approach.

For GATT-inconsistent trade restrictions in qualifying IEAs, special exceptions would then be available:

- In the waiver scenario, the basic voting procedure would apply, but a longer time-frame for a waiver could be provided, with less stringent review requirements. These elements could even be determined on a case-by-case basis, once again being tailored to the specific IEA.
- In the Article XX scenario, similar flexibility could be built in. Indeed, it would be open for consideration whether the trade provisions of listed IEAs could enjoy an indefinite exception, perhaps subject to periodic review.
- In either approach, we would need to consider limiting GATT/WTO non-violation dispute settlement rights of a non-party to the IEA in cases where the trade restrictions in question represent sanctions aimed at obtaining their participation (thereby limiting the prospect of compensation for the nullification of trade benefits otherwise accruing to the non-party). Presumably, it would be counterproductive to apply trade restrictions designed to impose economic pressure and then to offset the impact of the restrictions by allowing for compensation. However, developing countries in particular could resist this element.

Responding to the Trading Agenda

As indicated in previous sections, there is potential for serious trade disruption arising from the use of certain trade-related environmental measures, such as eco-labelling, packaging, recycling and disposal requirements, taxes and so on. These issues need to be urgently addressed. It is still too early to suggest specific options, however. We are still in an analytical phase, identifying the nature and extent of the problem. Considerable homework needs to be done by participants in the GATT/WTO process to flesh out the multilateral picture, as well as domestically to clarify national positions regarding the local use of the measures in question and their impact on exports when used by others. Although there exists a general assessment of where interests lie, with the most serious implications arising on the export side of the equation, more work needs to be done to focus on key problems and the best solutions.

We should bear in mind throughout the analytical work that is underway, and that should be stepped up under the new GATT/WTO work programme, the likely need to improve disciplines, and compliance with those disciplines, through interpretations of and possibly amendments to the relevant GATT/WTO Articles and Agreements. Progress in the GATT/WTO will depend to some extent on progress in the development of common standards or programmes in the relevant fora. Work in the WTO should be coordinated with, and could help to accelerate, these related activities.

CONCLUSIONS

AS WAS INDICATED AT THE BEGINNING OF THIS PAPER, the trade and environment debate is ultimately about the best means to pursue improved environmental protection. Those who closely follow environmental issues know better than most that the pace of progress can be frustratingly slow. The problems are often complex and the science uncertain. There are sometimes commercial objectives tangled up in environmental measures. And different countries have different priorities and capacities to address competing demands. Indeed, some developing countries have virtually no capacity to respond to the environmental agenda being pressed upon them. At the end of the day, costs will be high, something that most taxpayers, including in the developed world, are not yet prepared to absorb fully.

There are no magic answers, least of all in the GATT/WTO. The challenge is to look for approaches that are feasible, that will make a lasting contribution to progress and that will not end up doing more harm than good.

The trading system can and does, in fact, play an important supporting role. Trade is one of the central forces driving international economic growth, which in turn is a critical factor in advancing the goal of environmental protection. The evidence is clear that an open, predictable and non-discriminatory trade regime is a prerequisite for increased wealth, which is a prerequisite for a better environment. Changing the rules to allow for easier use of discriminatory and extraterritorial trade restrictions may have short-term appeal for some, but it would be counterproductive for the trading system in the long-run. Denying export opportunities, especially to developing countries, would simply eliminate a source of the income necessary to deal with an environmental problem. It also would undermine the international trust and cooperation that will be necessary for long-term success —few governments would tolerate for long such intrusions into their domestic jurisdiction through the use of trade penalties by others. Such an approach would, moreover, invite protectionist abuse.

There undoubtedly will be much debate over these issues. Nonetheless, one thing is clear—while the GATT/WTO can provide support in a number of ways, including by ensuring that the trade rules do not get in the way of decisions by the international community on environmental policy and programmes, it cannot itself make or arbitrate those decisions. Nor should it be called upon to enforce or police environmental standards or programmes that have not been accepted internationally. This approach is neither desirable nor negotiable. After all, the GATT/WTO is nothing more than an organization bringing together for trade purposes the same governments that gather in other organizations for environmental purposes. Those that are not yet in a position to agree on environmental issues in environmental fora are unlikely to agree in the GATT/WTO on the use of trade penalties to enforce those issues.

The role in the GATT/WTO, therefore, should be support and

non-interference, not intervention; fine tuning the interface between environmental programmes and the trade rules, not creating blunt instruments. Ultimately, the WTO should be left to do what it is mandated to do and, in fact, does best —liberalize and regulate trade, which, over time, will be its most important contribution to future generations.

FOOTNOTES

1. Canada agreed to have a fine levied in such circumstances made enforceable through the domestic courts.
2. This dynamic was in fact present from the inception of the Montreal Protocol and is a key to its success. With OECD countries responsible for over 90% of world production and consumption of the chemicals in question and agreed on a schedule for phasing them out, there was little market scope related to these products for developing countries. With the only meaningful sources of supply or export markets disappearing, developing countries could not continue to produce the controlled chemicals unless production was entirely for domestic consumption. In this case, measures linked to trade in those chemicals or goods containing them would have had no effect in any event. Given the realities of the situation, the positive incentives of longer phase-out periods as well as access to financial and technical assistance to help cope with the changing conditions internationally were probably much more meaningful in encouraging the adherence of non-parties than trade sanctions. As a practical matter, these appear superfluous. The sometimes stated objective of banning trade with non-parties to prevent shifts in production also appears dubious. It is not trade in the chemicals themselves that could lead to relocation of production. On the contrary, cutting off supply would be more likely to lead to new or increased production in countries that decided to continue domestic use of the controlled chemicals. Prohibiting the transfer of technology and equipment would be more relevant, but there is no such requirement in the Protocol. Article 4(5) comes closest: "Each Party undertakes to the fullest practicable extent possible to discourage the export to any State not party to this Protocol of technology for producing and for utilizing controlled substances."
3. It is worth noting here that parties could agree to the use of GATT-inconsistent measures amongst themselves, although in any such case the measures should be spelled out and clearly understood. In the event of a dispute, parties would have recourse to their GATT rights. As a practical matter, however, if the dispute arose because the pro-

vision in the IEA was unclear or there was no understanding on implementation at the national level, that would reflect shortcomings in the IEA itself. It is unlikely that the GATT would be the appropriate forum to address those shortcomings (e.g., a GATT panel would not undertake to interpret the provisions of another treaty). This highlights the need for well-developed dispute settlement provisions applying to parties in the IEA itself. For a more detailed discussion of these issues, see Keith H. Christie, "Stacking the Deck: Compliance and Dispute Settlement in International Environmental Agreements," Department of Foreign Affairs and International Trade, Policy Staff Paper No.93/15 (December 1993) (included in this volume).
4. For Canada, the ITAC/SAGIT structure provides the basis for such consultation. The new International Trade Advisory Committee (ITAC) Task Force on trade and environment will be a critical element in the domestic consultative process.
5. Beyond those goods covered by a recent decision of the Parties to the Basel Convention on the Transboundary Movement of Hazardous Wastes.
6. See also the discussion in Christie, "Stacking the Deck."

V

Robert T. Stranks

The New Jerusalem: Globalization, Trade Liberalization and Some Implications for Canadian Labour Policy

... the concept of the determinant socio-economic environment injects a completely new and much more comprehensive dimension into policy-making, emphasizing the need to take into consideration a broader spectrum of policy domains and to implement cross-disciplinary approaches.[1]

The issue is not only one of wages, but how far Canadian attempts to improve working conditions more generally will be constrained or even undone by the increasing competition with the U.S. and other countries for investment and sales.[2]

The Canadian economy is undergoing profound and continuous structural changes that are likely to intensify in the remainder of the 1990s. These changes are re-ordering the basis of economic activity across a range of industries. Our economic future increasingly will be enhanced by our ability to develop our knowledge and skills to generate new ideas and to transform these ideas into new products and processes.[3]

INTRODUCTION

IT IS WIDELY RECOGNIZED THAT NATIONAL ECONOMIES are becoming more interdependent and integrated. With this development, the distinction between domestic and international policies is becoming increasingly blurred. In all likelihood, the post-Uruguay Round international trade policy agenda will be extremely complex and broad in scope. What has traditionally been considered "trade policy," such as issues associated with tariffs, industrial policy, voluntary export restraints, government procurement and trade remedy law, will constitute only a part of the post-Round agenda. The Uruguay Round's agenda broke from the past by considering such issues as trade in services, trade-related investment measures and trade-related intellectual property rights. In the future, if the current high level of political interest continues, multilateral negotiations will encompass trade-environment linkages, trade-competition linkages and trade-labour issues. The fundamental reason for the broadening of the trade policy mandate is the global move toward more market-oriented economies, and the growing realization that domestic policies may affect trade.

This paper is concerned with the trade and foreign direct investment dimension of globalization and its implications for Canadian labour policies, principally in the manufacturing sector. In particular, it briefly considers what pressure globalization may bring to bear on labour market adjustment, and how labour rights are addressed in the North American Agreement on Labour Cooperation (NAALC) between the Canada, the U.S. and Mexico. The paper then considers if there is a need to address labour and trade issues in a broader international context, and how a multilateral dialogue or negotiation might begin to approach the issue.

GLOBALIZATION[4]

What is Globalization

"Globalization" was first referred to by Theodore Levitt as the emergence of global markets for standardized consumer products with global firms producing for these markets.[5] The term has now taken on a broader meaning and refers to increasing levels of economic interdependence and integration. Globalization is now understood to mean a process that involves the increasing cross-national spread of products, markets, firms and production factors.[6] In the globalization process, national boundaries are becoming less relevant to the conduct of business. Globalization is not confined to export industries. Import-competing industries are equally, although perhaps less obviously, a part of the global marketplace. International trade flows and foreign direct investment are indicators of globalization.

Globalization and Trade

Increased economic interdependence is reflected in the annual growth in the volume of world trade. Increases in the volume of world merchandise trade have outpaced the growth of world output in goods (Chart 1). Firms are exporting an increasing share of their production to foreign markets.

Chart 1
Volume of World Merchandise,
Trade and Output 1960–1991

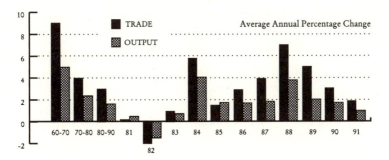

There is also evidence to suggest that international trade in services has at least kept pace with growth in trade in goods and, therefore, has also outpaced growth rates of world output in goods. Trade in services is also contributing to a more interdependent global economy.[8]

The geographic pattern of trade highlights some broad features of interdependence. The largest part of the OECD countries' exports, approximately 74 per cent, is amongst themselves, rather than between these countries and the developing countries.[9] Intraregional exports are also important, with trade within Western Europe accounting for 72 per cent of its total exports in 1991 (Table 1).[10] On balance, the traditional pattern of developed countries exporting manufactured goods to the developing countries, and the developing countries exporting primary products is still evident. Nonetheless, the developing countries' exports of manufactured goods are a fast-growing part of world trade. Yet the distribution of developing country exports remains skewed. Most of the developing countries' growth in manufactured goods is accounted for by the newly industrializing economies (NIEs), especially those in East Asia, as well as Mexico and Brazil.

Table 1
Shares of Intra-regional exports in total merchandise exports of regions, 1986-91
(Per centage)

	1986	1987	1988	1989	1990	1991*
North America	39.1	37.8	35.4	34.2	34.3	33.0
Latin America	14.0	13.8	13.4	14.1	13.4	16.0
Western Europe	68.4	70.5	70.6	70.7	72.2	72.4
C./E. Europe and former USSR	53.3	52.7	52.0	48.5	42.8	22.4
Africa	5.9	6.7	7.0	6.6	5.9	6.6
Middle East	7.7	6.9	6.9	6.3	5.8	5.1
Asia	37.0	38.8	41.8	44.1	44.8	46.7

* Intra-regional shares are affected by the unification of Germany and major changes in the valuation of the trade of Central and Eastern Europe and the former USSR. Source: GATT

Foreign Direct Investment and The Global Firm

A second key indicator of globalization is private sector direct investment. While governments may facilitate or hinder globalization, the global firm is the key player in the globalization process. Foreign direct investment (FDI) is not simply an international transfer of capital, it is also an extension of a firm, including some degree of its entrepreneurial and management skills, into a foreign country. Global firms are enterprises that have adopted global corporate strategies to increase their efficiency. Global firms establish production facilities on an international basis, pursue strategic alliances with foreign firms and obtain inputs for production internationally. The degree to which firms have become "stateless," however, can easily be exaggerated.[11] Much research and development is done in the home country, and consortia are often established among firms from the same region. Needless to say, there is a trend toward a greater level of cross-border business activities, but the "stateless" firm is more of a myth than a reality, at least to date.

An important aspect of the global and regional pattern of production is foreign direct investment. Growth in the stock of FDI was exceptionally strong in the 1985-1990 period, increasing at an average annual rate of 19.4 per cent. This slowed in 1991 to 11.2 per cent.[12] From 1985 to 1991, the world stock of FDI increased from US $733 billion to US $1,882 billion. An interesting and important feature of FDI is that most of the investment occurs within the developed countries. In 1967, the developed countries accounted for 69.4 per cent of the world stock of inward direct investment, and 76.6 per cent in 1991 (Table 2).[13] The perception that most FDI, or even an increasing proportion, is flowing from the developed to the developing countries is incorrect. On a regional basis, however, the Asian developing countries have seen a remarkable increase in foreign inward investment during the 1980-91 period, increasing from 7.1 per cent to 14.3 per cent of the global total.

Table 2
World Stock of Inward Direct Investment in Major Host Countries or Regions, Selected Years, 1967-91
(Billions of Dollars or Per centage)

	Amount				Per cent Distribution			
	1967	1973	1980	1991	1967	1973	1980	1991
All Countries	105.5	208.1	505.3	1,882.7	100.0	100.0	100.0	100.0
Developed Countries	73.2	153.7	394.1	1,442.7	69.4	73.9	78.0	76.6
United States	9.9	20.6	83.0	414.4	9.4	9.9	16.4	22.0
Europe	31.4	79.9	211.6	807.5	29.8	38.4	41.9	42.9
EC(12)	24.8	68.0	186.9	714.2	23.5	32.7	37.0	37.9
Other Europe	6.6	12.0	24.7	93.2	6.3	5.8	4.9	5.0
Sweden	0.5	1.0	1.7	15.8	0.5	0.5	0.3	0.8
Switzerland	2.1	4.3	14.3	44.2	2.0	2.1	2.8	2.3
Other European Countries	4.0	6.7	8.7	33.2	3.8	3.2	1.7	1.8
CANADA	19.2	33.0	51.6	113.9	18.2	15.9	10.2	6.0
Australia and New Zealand	4.9	10.5	28.1	83.7	4.6	5.0	5.6	4.4
SouthAfrica	7.2	8.1	16.5	11.1	6.8	3.9	3.3	0.6
Japan	0.6	1.6	3.3	12.3	0.6	0.8	0.7	0.7
Developing Countries	32.3	54.4	111.2	440.0	30.6	26.1	22.0	23.4
Western Hemisphere	18.5	28.9	62.3	132.1	17.5	13.9	12.3	7.0
Africa	5.6	10.2	13.1	38.8	5.3	4.9	2.6	2.1
Asia	8.3	15.3	35.8	269.1	7.9	7.4	7.1	14.3
Middle East	3.2	4.3	4.3	12.3	3.0	2.1	0.9	0.7
Other Asian Countries	5.1	11.0	31.5	256.7	4.8	5.3	6.2	13.6
Addenda:								
Outward Stock	112.3	211.1	516.9	1,836.5				
Inward Stock	105.5	208.1	505.3	1,882.7				
Difference	6.8	3.0	11.6	-46.2				
OPEC Countries	8.2	13.8	10.8	31.9	7.8	6.6	2.1	1.7

NOTE: Detail may not add to totals because of rounding. End of year exchange rates were used to convert stocks valued in local currencies to U.S. dollars.
Source: John Rutter, "Recent Trends in International Direct Investment: The Boom Years Fade," U.S. Department of Commerce, August 1993.

Foreign direct investment is undertaken for a number of reasons. Graham Vickery[14] has set out five major objectives motivating FDI. These are: to facilitate the penetration of foreign markets, to take advantage of the opportunities provided by technological change, to secure a presence in all major centres of production and consumption, to keep costs down and to increase global flexibility in production and distribution. In deciding where to locate new investment, these motivating objectives, as well as a number of related factors such as the reliability of transportation and communications networks, political stability and social considerations, are taken into account by firms. For the purpose of this Paper, it is worth noting that labour, or access to low cost labour, is but one of a number of factors influencing a firm's decision to undertake FDI in any particular location.

While the benefits of foreign direct investment for host countries, such as employment, enhanced access to technology and intensified competition, are widely recognized, it is less often recognized that foreign direct investment by domestic firms, i.e., outward direct investment, may also have positive effects on domestic employment. Foreign investment by domestic firms can create employment by raising exports of capital goods and, in the long run, by influencing demand for domestically produced intermediate components, replacement parts and associated goods and services.[15] Economic growth in the recipient country may also increase the demand for products from the FDI source country.

TRADE LIBERALIZATION

The Economic Benefits of Trade Liberalization

The economic benefits of trade liberalization are widely recognized, whether carried out unilaterally, bilaterally or multilaterally. By allowing the optimal allocation of factors of production, trade is an important contributor to economic growth. Trade allows countries to move beyond their national production possibility frontiers, and in so doing to enjoy a higher standard of living than would otherwise have been the case.

The benefits derived from trade liberalization arise from several sources. The reduction or elimination of barriers to trade encourages countries to produce and trade goods in which they have a comparative advantage. Trade liberalization also allows for the greater exploitation of economies of scale. By allowing domestic producers greater market access opportunities, the freer market conditions allow firms to undertake greater specialized production runs that reduce the unit costs of production. For countries with small domestic markets, economies of scale may be extremely important.

Trade liberalization also increases competition, in both the foreign and domestic markets. This implies that firms will need to respond faster to changing market conditions. Greater competition is likely to provide an incentive for firms to increase their economic performance through cost-saving innovations and to enhance the quality of their products. Trade liberalization undertaken in a bilateral or multilateral context and which establishes clear trading rules will reduce uncertainty. Without such rules, a country may face unilateral actions from its trade partners. The reduction of uncertainty, while providing more stable access, will also allow firms to make more informed business decisions.

Labour Adjustment

The economic benefits stemming from trade liberalization require adjustment, including labour market adjustment. The OECD has summarized the empirical results of a number of studies conducted on the employment effects of trade liberalization.[16] The OECD concluded that the net impact of trade liberalization on employment is in general small at the aggregate level of the overall economy. The labour adjustment required is also likely to be small with respect to changes occurring for other reasons, such as technological change or the emergence of new products. In an average year in the developed countries, 20 per cent of the work force will change jobs. The OECD report concluded that "the number of additional workers who would have to change jobs as a result of trade liberalization would be likely to be only a fraction of the normal rate of labour turnover, particularly if the trade liberalization were spread over a number of years."[17]

The employment effect is more important, however, at the sectoral level, although smaller than employment changes due to other causes, such as large exchange rate movements and technological developments. The OECD has found that trade liberalization and increased trade in goods, especially with developing countries, tends to intensify structural change in the OECD countries through a labour-saving effect that reduces demand for unskilled workers, while stimulating demand for skilled workers. On a sectoral basis, employment in low-wage and low-technology industries in the OECD countries in general is adversely affected by imports, while high-wage and high-technology industries experience gains in employment.[18] The OECD also noted that social "problems may arise if the job displacements tend to concentrate on groups of the labour force who are disadvantaged anyway, e.g., unskilled labour."[19] From a political perspective, highly visible and concentrated sectoral job losses may not be offset by the more diffuse job gains.

Disciplines on Traditional Policy Response Instruments

Since the establishment of the GATT, tariffs in the developed countries have fallen greatly. Their unweighted averages, which was around 40 per cent, is now 5 per cent, or lower.[20] The conclusion of the Uruguay Round, where the participants have agreed to more than a one-third cut in tariffs, will further reduce the level of protection of both the developed and developing countries. In the case of the European Union (EU), intra-EU tariffs have been eliminated, and for Canada and the U.S. tariff reductions are proceeding under the tiered phase-out of the Canada-United States Free Trade Agreement (FTA). The North American Free Trade Agreement will also reduce and eventually eliminate tariffs vis-à-vis Mexico. Progress has also been made on reducing non-tariff barriers, such as government procurement policies that treat domestic suppliers preferentially. Multilaterally or regionally agreed to reductions in non-tariff measures and the tightening of trade rules, such as new disciplines on the use of countervailing and anti-dumping measures, will further promote cross-border flows of goods and services.

While trade liberalization promotes competition, increased integration also creates adjustment pressures. This has implications for domestic labour policies. With integration, the use of trade policy instruments and trade distorting domestic measures, such as subsidization, while not prohibited, is constrained.

Protectionist trade policy instruments and subsidization have the effect of raising the relative price of imports in order to reduce competitive pressure on import-competing domestic firms. Progressive trade liberalization, such as the binding and reductions of tariffs in successive GATT rounds, has reduced the ability of countries to protect domestic producers. With bound tariffs, firms have much less political leverage to pressure governments into raising tariffs in response to foreign competition. With increased levels of integration, i.e., fewer tariff and non-tariff barriers, labour adjustment policies in response to increased competition take on greater importance. Countries no longer have the same range of policy options to delay or avoid adjustment. This is true for all countries participating in economic integration. For Canada, it is important to realize that authorities in Canada's export markets are also constrained from mobilizing the full range of measures previously available to protect their local producers from Canadian competitors.

The successful conclusion of the Uruguay Round includes new disciplines on trade-related intellectual property (TRIPS) such as patents, copyrights and trademarks, and trade-related investment measures (TRIMS). TRIMS include such measures as local content requirements that specify that the production process must use a certain proportion of inputs that are produced in the host country, and export performance requirements that specify that a firm must maintain a minimum volume or value of exports. Multilateral discipline on TRIMS in particular will influence business decisions on the location of investment and production. The prohibition of several TRIMS removes certain government imposed constraints that may negatively affect investment. Consequently, by establishing effective multilateral rules on TRIPS and TRIMS within a trade agreement, policy flexibility in these areas is reduced in both import and export markets.

CANADA: A SMALL, OPEN, TRADE DEPENDENT ECONOMY

Canada and Trade

The cornerstone of Canadian trade policy has been active support for the liberalization of the international trading system via rulemaking, most particularly through the establishment of the GATT and successive GATT rounds, as well as regionally through the FTA and the North American Free Trade Agreement (NAFTA). Canada has a relatively small domestic market. Maintaining and enhancing access to foreign markets is vital to the Canadian economy and improving Canadian living standards. Exports are one of the main sources of economic growth and job creation in Canada. Canadian exports of C$ 156 billion[21] in 1992 are equivalent to roughly 25 per cent of GDP. This is over twice the percentage of the U.S. and Japan.[22]

Canada's trade relations with the U.S. are particularly important. Roughly 75 per cent of Canadian exports are destined for the U.S. market, while imports from the U.S. account for about 70 per cent of all Canadian imports. The Canada-United States Free Trade Agreement lowered barriers to trade between the two countries, extended trade liberalization to areas such as services, which did not then fall within the mandate of the GATT, and established a more effective dispute settlement mechanism. While arguably the FTA did not increase Canada's economic interdependence on a global basis, it did increase the level of regional economic integration.

For Canada, the NAFTA increased market access opportunities in Mexico and the U.S., and prevented a hub-and-spoke model of regional trade arrangements from developing. In a hub-and-spoke model, the U.S. would negotiate free trade agreements with other countries or groups of countries separately. In such an environment, investment would tend to flow to the U.S. from where firms could trade freely with all the U.S. bilateral trading partners. The NAFTA ensures Canada remains an attractive location for foreign and domestic investment, but the prospect of a hub-and-spoke model developing with the U.S. at the centre will arise in the context of how free trade arrangements evolve in the Western Hemisphere. In this regard, an important element of the NAFTA is its provision that other countries may become parties to the free trade area, an important feature proposed by Canada.

Analytical research suggests that the NAFTA has three main implications for Canadian labour.[23] These are broadly consistent with the nature of the findings of the OECD study discussed earlier in this Paper.

- The aggregate number of jobs created or lost is likely to be relatively small, at least for the foreseeable future.
- Even if the net employment effect is not large, there will be employment loss in some sectors. Job loss will pose adjustment problems for Canadians whose skills, age and educational levels mismatch them for emerging employment opportunities in more highly skilled areas.
- The overall employment effect could lead to some intensification of wage polarization, unless worker retraining programmes are appropriately modernized and given a clearer focus. Canadians best situated to benefit from the increased market access to Mexico will be highly-skilled and highly-paid "knowledge" workers.

Canada and Inward and Outward Direct Investment[24]

Canada has an open policy towards inward foreign direct investment. The total stock of foreign direct investment in Canada in 1992 was C$ 136.6 billion (Table 3).[25] Canada's sources of foreign direct investment are becoming more diversified. During the early 1950s, the U.S. accounted for 86 per cent of Canada's total stock of foreign direct investment.

Table 3
Foreign Direct Investment in Canada by Selected Countries

Year	United States	United Kingdom	Germany	France	Other Europe	Japan	Hong Kong	Other Countries	Total
				($ Billions)					
1960	11.2	1.6	0.1	0.1	0.5	—	—	0.1	13.6
1970	22.1	2.6	0.4	0.5	1.4	0.1	—	0.3	27.4
1980	50.4	5.8	1.8	1.3	3.5	0.6	0.1	1.2	64.7
1981	53.8	6.6	2.0	1.3	4.2	1.0	0.1	1.3	70.3
1982	54.5	7.1	2.0	1.4	4.9	1.3	0.1	1.5	72.8
1983	58.4	7.8	1.9	1.3	4.1	1.6	0.1	2.2	77.4
1984	63.4	8.2	2.1	1.3	4.6	1.8	0.2	1.8	83.4
1985	66.0	8.5	2.2	1.5	5.0	1.9	0.2	1.9	87.2
1986	67.0	11.2	2.5	1.7	4.8	2.3	0.4	2.5	92.4
1987	71.8	12.7	3.1	1.8	5.5	2.5	0.6	3.8	101.8
1988	73.7	16.1	3.4	2.2	6.9	3.1	1.0	4.1	110.5
1989	78.2	16.4	3.6	3.5	8.3	4.1	1.1	3.8	119.0
1990	80.9	18.0	4.9	3.9	9.3	4.1	1.3	4.2	126.6
1991	83.8	17.1	5.2	3.9	10.3	5.3	2.3	3.7	131.6
1992	87.3	17.1	N/A	N/A	N/A	5.6	N/A	N/A	136.6
				(% of Total)					
1960	82.3	11.7	0.7	0.7	3.9	—	—	0.7	100.0
1970	80.7	9.5	1.5	1.8	5.1	0.4	—	1.0	100.0
1980	77.9	9.0	2.8	2.0	5.4	0.9	0.2	1.8	100.0
1981	76.5	9.4	2.8	1.8	6.0	1.4	0.1	2.0	100.0
1982	74.9	9.8	2.7	1.9	6.7	1.8	0.1	2.1	100.0
1983	75.5	10.1	2.5	1.7	5.3	2.1	0.1	2.8	100.0
1984	76.0	9.8	2.5	1.6	5.5	2.2	0.2	2.2	100.0
1985	75.7	9.7	2.5	1.7	5.7	2.2	0.2	2.2	100.0
1986	73.1	12.1	2.7	1.8	5.2	2.5	0.4	2.7	100.0
1987	70.5	12.5	3.0	1.8	5.4	2.5	0.6	3.7	100.0
1988	66.7	14.6	3.1	2.0	6.2	2.8	0.9	3.7	100.0
1989	65.7	13.8	3.0	2.9	7.0	3.4	0.9	3.2	100.0
1990	63.9	14.2	3.9	3.1	7.3	3.2	1.0	3.3	100.0
1991	63.7	13.0	4.0	3.0	7.8	4.0	1.7	2.8	100.0
1992	63.9	12.5	N/A	N/A	N/A	4.1	N/A	N/A	100.0

N/A - Not Available
Source: Statistics Canada

This figure has gradually decreased. Since 1990, the U.S. has accounted for approximately 64 per cent of the total stock. During the past ten years, the United Kingdom, France, Germany, Japan and Hong Kong have increased their shares.

Canada has an open policy for investing abroad. The stock of direct Canadian investment abroad in 1992 was C$ 99 billion (Table 4).[26] Changes in Canadian direct investment abroad has not been as pronounced as changes in foreign direct investment in Canada. The U.S. remains the major destination of Canadian investment abroad, accounting for about 58 per cent of total investment abroad as of 1992. On the other hand, the United Kingdom, France and Japan have increased their share of total Canadian investment abroad since 1984. For Canada, the relatively high-wage developed countries remain the major source and destination of direct investment.

An Overview of Canadian Labour Law

Canadian labour policy is covered by a wide range of labour laws. The major fields are industrial relations, employment standards, occupational health and safety and workers' compensation. Yet it is an over-simplification to speak of Canadian labour law or policies. In Canada, the provinces have extensive constitutional responsibilities for labour legislation. The jurisdiction of the federal and provincial governments arise from the Constitution Act, 1867, Sections 91 and 92. Judicial interpretation of these sections gives provincial legislatures major jurisdiction, while the federal government is responsible for labour affairs with respect to a much more limited range of industries, such as air transport and the banks. The complexity of Canadian labour law is further exacerbated by the many differences among the provinces' labour laws. The provinces are far from having harmonized labour standards.[27]

The following gives some appreciation of the range of issues dealt with in each of the labour-related fields.

- Industrial relations are concerned with the acquisition of bargaining rights by trade unions, the conditions for exercising the right to strike, strike replacements and reinstatement of striking employees, and union security.

Table 4
Canadian Direct Investment Abroad by Selected Countries

Year	United States	United Kingdom	Germany	France	Other Europe	Japan	Hong Kong	Other Countries	Total
				($ Billions)					
1960	1.6	0.3	—	—	—	—	0.1	0.4	2.4
1970	3.3	0.6	0.1	0.1	0.3	—	0.2	1.6	6.2
1980	16.8	2.9	0.3	0.3	1.3	0.1	0.7	4.6	27.0
1981	22.4	3.0	0.3	0.3	1.7	0.1	1.0	5.0	33.8
1982	23.8	2.8	0.3	0.2	1.9	0.1	1.0	5.5	35.6
1983	26.6	3.0	0.3	0.2	2.1	0.2	1.0	6.5	39.9
1984	32.2	3.4	0.4	0.1	2.5	0.2	1.0	7.6	47.4
1985	37.1	4.0	0.5	0.2	3.1	0.2	1.0	8.0	54.1
1986	39.4	4.6	0.6	0.4	3.1	0.2	1.1	9.1	58.5
1987	43.4	6.2	0.7	0.6	3.7	0.2	1.3	10.7	66.8
1988	46.5	7.1	0.7	1.5	3.2	0.4	1.8	10.9	72.1
1989	50.3	9.3	0.8	1.7	4.5	0.4	2.1	11.7	80.8
1990	52.8	11.3	0.8	1.7	5.6	0.8	2.3	12.6	87.9
1991	54.6	12.3	0.9	1.7	6.4	1.7	2.1	14.7	94.4
1992	57.8	10.9	N/A	N/A	N/A	1.8	N/A	N/A	99.0
				(% of Total)					
1960	66.7	12.5	—	—	—	—	4.2	16.6	100.0
1970	53.2	9.7	1.6	1.6	4.8	—	3.2	25.9	100.0
1980	62.2	10.7	1.1	1.1	4.8	0.4	2.6	17.1	100.0
1981	66.3	8.9	0.9	0.9	5.0	0.3	3.0	14.7	100.0
1982	66.9	7.9	0.8	0.6	5.3	0.3	2.8	15.4	100.0
1983	66.7	7.5	0.8	0.5	5.2	0.5	2.5	16.3	100.0
1984	67.9	7.2	0.8	0.2	5.2	0.4	2.1	16.2	100.0
1985	68.6	7.4	0.9	0.4	5.7	0.4	1.8	14.8	100.0
1986	67.3	7.9	1.0	0.7	5.3	0.3	1.9	15.6	100.0
1987	65.0	9.3	1.0	0.9	5.5	0.3	1.9	16.1	100.0
1988	64.4	9.8	1.1	2.0	4.4	0.6	2.5	15.2	100.0
1989	62.2	11.5	1.0	2.1	5.6	0.5	2.6	14.5	100.0
1990	60.1	12.9	1.0	1.9	6.4	0.9	2.6	14.2	100.0
1991	57.8	13.0	1.0	1.8	6.8	1.8	2.2	15.6	100.0
1992	58.4	11.0	N/A	N/A	N/A	1.8	N/A	N/A	100.0

N/A - Not Available
Source: Statistics Canada

- Employment standards are concerned with minimum wages, hours of work and overtime pay, general holidays with pay, annual paid vacations, maternity pay and equal pay.

- Occupational health and safety obligations, rights and standards refer to the right to refuse dangerous work, regulations for health and safety committees, and the right to know of physical or health safety hazards.
- Workers' compensation addresses compensation for workers or their dependents in respect of occupational accidents or diseases.[28]

The North American Agreement on Labour Cooperation

The overall objective of the North American Agreement on Labour Cooperation (NAACL)[29] is to give effect to the labour related commitments expressed in the Preamble of the NAFTA: to "improve working conditions and living standards in their respective territories," and to "protect, enhance and enforce basic workers' rights."[30] An important dimension of the NAACL is that it increases cooperation and will promote greater understanding among the three countries on a range of labour issues. The objectives of the agreement are to: improve working conditions and living standards in each country; encourage cooperation to promote innovation and rising levels of productivity and quality; promote publication and exchange of information to enhance mutual understanding of each country's laws; oversee cooperative labour-related activities; promote compliance and the effective enforcement by each country of its labour laws; foster transparency in the administration of labour law; and promote a number of key labour principles.

The labour principles that Canada, Mexico and the U.S. are to promote, subject to each country's specific domestic laws, are set out in an annex to the agreement. The NAACL does not establish common minimum standards. The following are the guiding principles:

1. Freedom of association and protection of the right to organize.
2. The right to bargain collectively.
3. The right to strike.
4. Prohibition of forced labour.

5. Labour protection for children and young persons.
6. Minimum employment standards.
7. Elimination of employment discrimination.
8. Equal pay for women and men.
9. Prevention of occupational injuries and illnesses.
10. Compensation in cases of occupational injuries and illnesses.
11. Protection of migrant workers.

The North American Agreement on Labour Cooperation contains an enforcement mechanism without creating new trade barriers for Canada. The agreement is based on the domestic enforcement of domestic law, and respects each country's sovereignty as well as provincial jurisdiction. The agreement aims to settle disputes through cooperation, but where countries fail to enforce their own domestic labour standards and do not correct the problem, they may be subject to a fine paid into a special labour fund.

If a country fails to pay the fine, it is liable to ongoing enforcement action. In Canada's case, fines will be enforced by domestic courts. This reflects the view of the provinces, the federal government and business, who believed that trade sanctions are not needed to ensure the enforcement of labour standards in Canada. In the case of Mexico and the United States, the country or countries raising the dispute may suspend NAFTA benefits equivalent to the amount of the fine.

External Pressures for Labour Adjustment in Canada

Globalization and trade liberalization are changing the international economic environment. Canadian labour and firms will need to adjust to the changing environment if Canada is to prosper.[31] External pressures on Canadian firms and labour include:

- Trade liberalization commitments under the Canada-U.S. Free Trade Agreement and the North American Free Trade Agreement.

- The decline in tariffs and greater openness of markets that will result from the successful conclusion of the Uruguay Round.
- The pace of technological change, which has forced Canadian firms to adopt new technologies to remain competitive, and has forced workers to acquire new skills. Technological change may also reduce the number of employees needed to produce more.
- Continued competition from highly developed, high income areas, including Japan and the European Union member states.
- The decline in transportation costs, combined with easier access to labour in developing countries, and improvements in telecommunications, which have provided opportunities for Canadian firms to locate production facilities abroad or to subcontract operations to foreign firms.
- The rise of new competitors, particularly the newly industrialized economies such as South Korea, Hong Kong and Taiwan.
- The movement of the newly industrialized economies out of labour-intensive products and into more skill-and capital-intensive products, and their replacement in labour-intensive production by such countries as Malaysia, Thailand, Indonesia and the PRC.

THE GREAT DEBATE: LOW WAGES AND SOCIAL DUMPING/COUNTERVAIL

Introduction

In Canada, labour unions, some political parties and the public at large have articulated interest in the relative labour conditions in Canada's trading partners and their possible influences on the level and quality of domestic employment. The Canadian Federation of Labour (CFL) and the Canadian Labour Congress (CLC) are both concerned that low standards of labour rights or the lax enforcement of labour rights in foreign countries grant foreign producers an "unfair" commercial advantage. They also believe that low standards of labour rights are undesirable on moral grounds.[32]

The most direct expression of the labour movement's concern about the impact of trade liberalization on labour conditions first appeared in respect of the FTA. During the debate over freer trade with the U.S., Canadians were particularly interested in the competitive challenge posed by producers in U.S. States with "right-to-work" legislation. "Right-to-work" legislation allows individual States to prohibit agreements requiring membership in a labour organization as a condition of employment.[33] With the negotiation of a North American Free Trade Agreement, the Canadian interest shifted in part from U.S. to Mexican labour conditions. More generally, there has been a growing interest in the labour conditions in developing countries, principally the newly industrialized economies and Eastern Europe, and what this may mean for Canadian producers. The labour movement and parts of the Democratic and Republican parties in the U.S. have expressed similar concerns, as did labour activists in Europe at the time of Spanish and Portuguese accessions to the European Community and more recently in connection with EU efforts to expand economic relations with Eastern Europe.

Low-wages

The labour movement's concern with NAFTA was largely centred on relative wage rates and the possible implications this could have for Canadian workers. Wage differentials between Mexico and Canada are large, with Mexican wages about one-sixth or one-seventh of Canadian levels in comparable industries.[34] Interest in low wages in the Mexican case stems from the concern that low wages in that country may exert downward pressure on wages in Canada and that investment will flow to Mexico because of its lower labour costs. The second concern is two-fold: it is feared that *new* investment will flow to Mexico rather than to Canada, and that companies already in Canada will relocate to Mexico.

Canadian outward direct investment is thus a major concern of some labour interests and others. At a minimum, labour groups advocate that trade agreements should include a clause that obliges countries to set and enforce minimum labour rights or standards.

The focus on wages rates, while raising strong feelings of "unfairness" in the public, is somewhat misleading.[35] Wages, while a substantial part of the total compensation of a worker, do not account for all employer-employee expenditures, such as legally required or contractual health and dental benefits, and life insurance. There is considerable diversity of non-wage benefits across countries, and as a percentage share of total compensation. In 1992, wages as defined as pay for time worked, accounted for about 70 to 75 per cent of total compensation costs for production workers in the manufacturing sectors in Canada, the U.S. and the United Kingdom, but for less than 60 per cent in Japan, France, Germany and Italy (Table 5).[36] In Mexico, non-wage benefits and profit sharing, under which all firms must distribute 10 per cent of pretax profits to employees, are reported to add more than 70 per cent to base payroll expenses.[37]

Most importantly, low levels of total compensation or wages do not necessarily mean low cost production. If low compensation costs were the basis for low production costs in the manufacturing sector, Table 6 shows that Sri Lanka, with an hourly compensation cost of U.S. 35 cents, would be an economic powerhouse.[38] But Sri Lanka is not a major manufacturer. Wage differences reflect differentials in labour productivities between countries. Generally, i.e., except in protected sectors where labour and management benefit from economic rents, higher wages are a function of higher productivity. The economic basis for low wages in countries like Sri Lanka and Mexico are an abundance of labour and low productivity. Analysis conducted by the Department of Finance estimates that Canadian labour productivity in the manufacturing sector is 6.5 times higher than a Mexican worker's.[39]

Table 5
Pay for time worked as a percentage of hourly compensation costs for production workers in manufacturing, 29 countries or areas, selected years, 1975-92

Country or Area	1975	1980	1985	1987	1988	1989	1990	1991	1992
United States	75.9	73.7	73.3	73.3	73.3	73.2	72.6	71.7	70.8
Canada	81.8	79.4	77.6	77.2	77.1	77.2	76.6	75.9	75.2
Mexico	—	—	—	—	—	—	—	—	—
Australia	77.5	76.3	75.2	74.6	74.6	74.6	74.6	74.6	74.6
Hong Kong	—	—	—	—	—	—	—	—	—
Israel	—	—	—	—	—	—	—	—	—
Japan	59.6	59.2	59.3	59.5	59.2	58.6	58.2	58.1	58.4
Korea	—	—	—	—	—	—	—	—	—
New Zealand	81.6	81.6	81.6	81.6	81.6	81.6	81.6	81.6	81.6
Singapore	73.0	66.7	63.7	75.2	73.0	69.9	68.5	67.1	66.7
Sri Lanka	71.4	71.4	67.6	67.6	67.6	67.6	67.6	—	—
Taiwan	—	—	—	—	—	—	—	—	—
Austria	56.0	54.2	52.4	52.6	52.5	52.5	52.3	52.6	52.6
Belgium	60.0	56.5	54.7	52.9	52.9	52.7	52.9	52.9	52.6
Denmark	85.1	84.2	81.8	81.6	85.0	85.0	84.6	84.0	84.0
Finland	68.8	64.4	63.5	61.7	60.4	60.1	59.3	59.8	59.8
France	60.0	58.5	55.3	54.7	54.0	54.2	54.6	54.8	54.7
Germany	61.5	58.5	57.0	56.8	56.7	56.8	56.1	56.0	55.8
Greece	64.1	64.1	62.1	62.1	62.1	62.1	62.1	62.1	—
Ireland	80.8	78.5	74.2	74.4	74.3	74.3	74.4	74.3	74.3
Italy	50.0	54.3	53.3	52.4	51.9	50.6	50.4	50.9	51.4
Luxembourg	69.8	70.8	70.3	70.2	70.2	70.2	70.2	—	—
Netherlands	59.1	57.7	57.4	56.8	57.0	57.3	56.8	56.9	57.1
Norway	71.7	69.3	68.7	69.0	68.7	68.8	68.6	69.1	69.6
Portugal	—	—	—	—	—	—	—	—	—
Spain	—	—	—	—	—	—	—	—	—
Sweden	68.8	61.8	59.3	58.8	58.9	58.6	59.0	57.6	57.2
Switzerland	68.3	67.1	65.7	65.4	65.6	65.7	65.7	65.3	65.3
United Kingdom	78.9	72.1	73.8	73.6	73.6	73.6	73.1	71.8	71.8

Source: U.S. Department of Labor, Bureau of Labor Statistics, "International Comparisons of Hourly Compensation Costs of Production Workers in Manufacturing," Report 844, April 1993.

Table 6
Hourly compensation costs in U.S. dollars for production workers in manufacturing, 29 countries or areas and selected economic groups, selected years, 1975-92

Country or Area	1975	1980	1985	1987	1988	1989	1990	1991	1992
United States	$6.36	$9.87	$13.01	$13.52	$13.91	$14.32	$14.91	$15.60	$16.17
Canada	5.98	8.67	10.98	12.09	13.55	14.83	15.95	17.18	17.02
Mexico	1.44	2.18	1.58	1.01	1.25	1.48	1.64	1.95	2.35
Australia	5.58	8.41	8.14	9.40	11.28	12.33	12.89	13.36	12.94
Hong Kong	.76	1.51	1.73	2.09	2.40	2.79	3.20	3.58	3.89
Israel	2.25	3.79	4.06	6.34	7.67	7.69	8.55	8.79	—
Japan	3.00	5.52	6.34	10.79	12.63	12.49	12.74	14.55	16.16
Korea	.33	.97	1.25	1.65	2.30	3.34	3.88	4.39	4.93
New Zealand	3.21	5.33	4.47	6.77	8.19	7.80	8.33	8.36	7.91
Singapore	.84	1.49	2.47	2.31	2.67	3.15	3.78	4.39	5.00
Sri Lanka	.28	.22	.28	.30	.31	.31	.35	—	—
Taiwan	.40	1.00	1.50	2.26	2.82	3.53	3.95	4.39	5.19
Austria	4.34	8.57	7.27	13.08	13.92	13.59	17.01	17.39	19.65
Belgium	6.41	13.11	8.97	15.25	15.82	15.51	19.22	19.83	22.01
Denmark	6.28	10.83	8.13	14.61	15.19	14.49	17.96	18.26	20.02
Finland	4.61	8.24	8.16	13.44	15.59	16.67	20.74	20.57	18.69
France	4.52	8.94	7.52	12.29	12.95	12.54	15.23	15.26	16.88
Germany	6.35	12.33	9.60	17.02	18.28	17.75	21.88	22.62	25.94
Greece	1.69	3.73	3.66	4.61	5.22	5.49	6.71	6.82	—
Ireland	3.03	5.95	5.92	9.30	10.00	9.66	11.76	12.07	13.32
Italy	4.67	8.17	7.63	13.02	13.98	14.41	17.46	18.29	19.41
Luxembourg	6.35	11.98	7.72	13.05	13.80	13.56	16.37	—	—
Netherlands	6.58	12.06	8.75	15.14	15.83	15.04	18.29	18.42	20.72
Norway	6.77	11.59	10.37	16.79	18.45	18.29	21.47	21.63	23.2
Portugal	1.58	2.06	1.53	2.52	2.78	2.90	3.69	4.15	5.01
Spain	2.53	5.89	4.66	7.63	8.55	8.94	11.33	12.20	13.39
Sweden	7.18	12.51	9.66	15.12	16.82	17.52	20.93	22.15	24.23
Switzerland	6.09	11.09	9.66	17.08	17.98	16.70	20.83	21.69	23.26
United kingdom	3.37	7.56	6.27	9.09	10.61	10.56	12.71	13.76	14.69

Source: U.S. Department of Labor, Bureau of Labor Statistics, "International Comparisons of Hourly Compensation Costs of Production Workers in Manufacturing," Report 844, April 1993.

"Social Dumping" and "Social Countervail"

Besides relative wage rates, some opponents of the FTA and NAFTA have focussed on the related issue of "social dumping". "Social dumping" has many definitions, but it often refers to the idea that different (read "lower") labour rights or standards give producers in the exporting country a commercial advantage.[40] It is important to note that this definition is restricted to exports, and is most likely to be raised by import-competing domestic producers. "Social dumping" has also been used to refer to difficulties competing in a foreign market due to the lower labour standards of the domestic producers in that market. While a domestic political constituency on the latter has not yet arisen, such an occurrence cannot be precluded. The concept could also be applied to trade in services, which could broaden further the political constituency on the issue.[41]

It is difficult to accept "social dumping" in the normal, i.e., GATT, sense of the term dumping. Article VI of the GATT defines dumping as the process "... by which products of one country are introduced into the commerce of another country at less than the normal value of the products ...". Moreover, dumping "... is to be condemned if it causes or threatens material injury to an established industry in the territory of a contracting party or materially retards the establishment of a domestic industry."[42] In practical terms, this means that dumping is the sale by a firm of an imported product at a lower price than that for which the firm sold the good in the exporting market. In such a case, Article VI allows a country to levy antidumping duties on a dumped product if it causes injury to domestic producers. International trade law does not recognize cost differentials between producers as potentially creating dumping, unless a given producer sells a given good at different prices in the home and export markets. If the price of the good in both markets reflects the cost of production, there is no dumping.

Another distinction between "social dumping" and dumping in a GATT sense is that "social dumping" often is taken to refer to an action by government, while in the GATT dumping refers to an action by a private producer. Under the GATT, governments have no obligation to encourage domestic firms from not dumping or of preventing firms from doing so. Under "social dumping," the concern appears to be with actions, i.e., setting domestic labour rights or standards, taken by governments; or perhaps more appropriately, inaction by governments, i.e., the failure to enforcement labour rights. Analytically, this is a useful distinction. Wages, to a great extent, are properly and directly a component of costs controlled by firms. This is the level at which charges of "dumping" make some analytical sense, although, again, it is important to emphasize that dumping in the trade sense does not occur unless a firm manipulates its prices between markets.

But what of a government's failure to implement and enforce "adequate" labour rights? Is such a government failure not akin to a subsidy that might legitimately attract a "social countervail"? It has been asserted that such "social dumping" is a form of subsidization and that countervailing duties are an appropriate response.[43] Under current GATT rules, "low" labour rights or standards or the failure to enforce labour standards would not constitute a subsidy, but Parties to a trade-labour agreement might wish to consider expanding the definition to include labour practices. This, however, raises the extremely complex and larger question of whether or not differences in economic or social policies should be considered a form of subsidization.

The allegation that a country is engaged in practices that might merit a "social countervail" in an importing country is easy to make, but difficult to substantiate. In the first place, formal labour rights and standards are often high in developing countries (this is certainly the case in Mexico), and sometimes higher than in certain developed countries (a comparison of U.S. and Mexican labour law is revealing in this respect). In the second place, the relationship between labour rights and labour costs is not straight-forward. There is little convincing empirical evidence on the relationship. Gunderson concluded that the limited empirical evidence tends to suggest that in

Canada unions increase wage costs by approximately 10 to 25 per cent, but that some of the cost increase is effectively reduced by the positive productivity-enhancing effects of unions.[44] Servais also has found that the actual influence of labour legislation on costs is difficult to evaluate.[45] He cites the example that the adoption of standards for the protection of workers can result in major savings, by inter alia reducing the disruptions in production owing to the absence of workers, and reducing the need to train replacements. Edgren also reached the conclusion that "it is open to discussion to what extent adoption of the ... standards would affect production costs and hence the international competitiveness of export producers in low-wage countries."[46]

Nor does the existence of "lower" or "weaker" labour rights (whether formal, or in the sense of weaker enforcement) imply that wages or labour costs will not rise. Fields conducted an analysis on four newly industrialized economies (Singapore, Taiwan, Hong Kong and South Korea) which have not actively promoted labour rights and organized labour, and have experienced high rates of economic growth.[47] Fields found that increased demand for labour bid up wages as firms competed for the labour supply, and that real wage rates rose. He concluded that the experiences of the four economies "exhibit a common feature: although the institutional structure of industrial relations continues to restrict labour organizations and collective bargaining, labour market opportunities have been getting very much better."[48] This conclusion may, however, beg the question of what would have happened to real wage rates if "strong" labour rights were in place in these economies.[49]

Problems with Enforcement

In addition to the unclear relationship between labour rights and costs, empirical data is generally lacking on the question of enforcement of labour laws. Systematic files on enforcement are not kept by the International Labour Organization or any other international organization.[50] Such data is essential to any meaningful dialogue on labour rights or conditions, as it is often alleged that countries, for the most part the developing countries, while having relatively high labour rights in law, fail to enforce the law. In conducting preparatory work for the NAFTA negotiations, Labour Canada concluded that it is difficult to find objective information about the application of labour laws in other countries.[51]

The question of non-enforcement of labour laws is also complicated by difficulties in identifying why the non-enforcement occurs. Non-enforcement may occur as a conscious decision on the part of government, or as a result of a lack of resources to effectively enforce the law. In practice, the amount of resources to enforce the law may become extremely burdensome for a country. The U.S., by many standards one of the wealthiest countries in the world, is widely recognized as having millions of illegal workers. Presumably, the employment conditions of these workers are less than those of U.S. workers legally employed and beneficiaries of U.S. labour laws. The question of enforcement may well need to be addressed in terms of acceptable and unacceptable levels of non-enforcement given a particular country's resources. It is not clear how well several developed countries would fare in such a comparison. Moreover, few are likely to favour the extension of the discussion of labour rights and standards to include labour mobility issues (i.e., temporary workers/immigration), although the EU has long recognized and acted on this linkage within the common market.

LABOUR STRATEGIES FOR A GLOBAL ECONOMY

THE STRATEGIC OPTIONS FOR LABOUR IN CANADA and other developed countries fall into three general categories.[52]

- Attempt to restrict the international mobility of capital, so that it cannot "shop" for the lower labour cost location.
- Attempt to influence the cost of doing business in foreign countries through international organizing, the further extension of international labour standards, and multi-

national bargaining to help to ensure the enforcement of those standards.
- Accept the mobility of capital, and deal with the adjustment side through domestic labour market policies, particularly in light of differing levels of productivity.

With globalization, the first option faces strong opposition, on both political and economic grounds. It will not be considered further in this Paper as a viable option. The remaining two options are more feasible and practical options. For governments, the two options may be characterized as policy responses in the domestic and international arenas, and this will be explored further.

The International Arena: The GATT and the Need for an International Dialogue

The GATT defines the rights and obligations of contracting parties with respect to trade. There is very little in the GATT related to labour standards or labour rights. The single reference to labour is in Article XX, which states that import restrictions may be used against imports of products produced by prison labour. There may, however, be a basis for considering trade and labour linkages in the GATT. Article XXIX of the GATT obliges contracting parties to undertake to observe the general principles of certain chapters of the (stillborn) International Trade Organization, i.e., the Havana Charter. Article 7 of Chapter II of the Havana Charter includes the general principle that unfair labour conditions should be discouraged in member countries.[53] The article provides that:

The Members recognize that measures relating to employment must take fully into account the rights of workers under intergovernmental declarations, conventions and agreements. They recognize that all countries have a common interest in the achievement and maintenance of fair labour standards related to productivity, and thus in the improvement of wages and working conditions as productivity may permit. The Members recognize that unfair labour conditions, particularly in production for export, create difficulties in international trade, and, accordingly each member shall take whatever action may be appropriate and feasible to eliminate such conditions within its territory.[54]

For over forty years, the U.S. has been periodically interested in or lobbying for the inclusion of some form of labour standards provision in the GATT. In 1953, the U.S. made a proposal, which was similar to Article 7 of the Havana Charter, to include a labour standard clause in the GATT. The provision stated that unfair labour conditions "may create difficulties in international trade which nullify or impair benefits under this Agreement."[55] Unfair labour conditions were defined as the "maintenance of labour conditions below those which the productivity of the industry and economy at large would justify."[56]

During the preparatory phase of the Uruguay Round, November 1985 to September 1986, the U.S. also attempted to have labour standards included in the agenda for the new round of multilateral trade negotiations. The U.S. presented a proposal that the following language be included in the Ministerial Declaration determining the mandate of the Uruguay Round:

Ministers recognize that [the] denial of worker rights can impede attainment of the objectives of the GATT and can lead to trade distortions, thereby increasing pressures for trade restrictive measures. Accordingly, the negotiations should review the effect of denial of worker rights on contracting parties, and the relationship of worker rights to GATT articles and objectives and related instruments, and consider possible ways of dealing with worker rights issues in the GATT so as to ensure that expanded trade benefits all workers in all countries.[57]

This proposal was not acceptable to the countries participating in the preparatory discussions, and the Ministerial Declaration for the Uruguay Round does not include a reference to workers' rights or standards.

More recently, at the November 1987 meeting of the GATT Council, the U.S. requested the establishment of a GATT Working Party to study the relationship between trade and internationally recognized labour standards. The international labour standards proposed for examination were those relating to: freedom of association; freedom to organize and bargain collectively; freedom from forced or compulsory labour; a minimum age for the employment of children; and measures setting minimum standards in respect of conditions of work.[58] The U.S. request received support from most developed countries, including Canada, but was opposed by many developing countries who were concerned that the proposed working party might be used to question legitimate comparative advantage.

At the October 1990 meeting of the GATT Council, the U.S. decided to amend its terms of reference for the proposed working party. The amendment narrowed the international labour standards proposed for examination to the freedom of association, the freedom to organize and bargain collectively and freedom from compulsory labour.[59] The U.S. believed that the amendment would address the sensitivities expressed by the developing countries. However, the GATT Contracting Parties have not reached a consensus on the establishment of such a working party.

The U.S. Policy Approach to Trade and Labour

The potential of U.S. trade actions based on unilateral decisions may be the best argument in support of establishing an international dialogue on trade-labour issues. In the past decade, the U.S. appears to be the only country that has included labour standards or workers' rights provisions in its trade law. Since 1983, the U.S. has linked labour-related standards to four major trade-related laws. The effects of these trade-related measures on foreign countries' labour conditions, however, are a matter of subjective interpretation and debate.[60]

The Caribbean Basin Economic Recovery Act (CBERA) provides for additional trade preferences to selected Caribbean and Central American countries under certain conditions. One of these conditions is related to labour standards and indicates that the President must take into account the degree to which workers are afforded reasonable workplace conditions and enjoy the right to organize and bargain collectively.

The U.S. Generalized System of Preferences (GSP) allows duty free access for a number of products imported from the developing countries. GSP benefits are granted unilaterally and are not bound in the GATT. The GSP was amended in 1984 to require that developing countries wishing to retain eligibility for duty free access meet certain conditions. The labour condition requires that countries must be "taking steps" to afford "internationally recognized worker rights."[61] The law defines such worker rights as follows: the right of association; the rights to organize and bargain collectively; a prohibition on the use of any form of forced or compulsory labour; a minimum age for the employment of children; and acceptable conditions of work with respect to minimum wages, hours of work, and occupational safety and health. Under this law, the U.S. Government is obliged to remove GSP benefits if the aforementioned "steps" are not taken. Since 1984, a number of countries have lost their GSP status, at least temporarily, as a result of this provision (e.g., Romania, Nicaragua and Paraguay).

The Overseas Private Investment Corporation (OPIC), established in 1969, is a government agency which insures U.S. investors against political risks in developing countries. In 1985, when OPIC's mandate came up for renewal, an amendment was adopted that authorized OPIC to " ...insure, reinsure, guarantee or finance a project only if the country in which the project is undertaken is taking steps to adopt and implement laws that extend internationally recognized worker rights to workers in the country."[62] Countries which have had OPIC insurance suspended at some time include Chile, Liberia, Nicaragua, Romania, South Korea and Sudan.

The Omnibus Trade and Competitiveness Act of 1988 has potentially far reaching implications for trade and labour. The U.S. Trade Act's Section 301 authorizes the President to treat as an "unfair" trade practice the competitive advantage of any country derived from the denial of internationally recognized labour rights. The Act also sets out the principle negotiating objectives of the U.S. regarding workers' rights. These are: to promote respect for worker rights; to secure a review of the relationship of workers' rights and the GATT; and to adopt as a principle of the GATT that the denial of workers' rights should not be a means for a country or its industries to gain competitive advantage in international trade.[63]

The U.S. debate on labour in respect to NAFTA also reflects a growing political and public interest in the linkages between trade and labour. While a candidate, Clinton announced that a labour side agreement was a condition necessary for NAFTA. In part due to this conditionality, U.S. labour supported Clinton's presidential election campaign. Organized labour, however, was dissatisfied with the NAALC and participated in a broad coalition to defeat Congressional passage of the NAFTA. The clear implication of the NAFTA labour experience is that future bilateral or regional economic arrangements including the U.S. are likely to involve a labour dimension of some sort. It also means that there is likely to be increased U.S. political interest in addressing the trade and labour issue in a multilateral context.[64]

An Approach for Multilateral Negotiations

Canada should support further work internationally on labour rights and standards and their link to trade, primarily for three reasons. First, Canadian values favour the promotion of at least certain labour rights, including the prohibition of child or forced labour and the implementation of high work place safety standards. Secondly, the failure to enforce labour rights and standards can have an impact on production costs—although the extent of the impact is not at all clear. And thirdly, the blocking of work internationally that could lead to at least limited negotiations will only encourage the U.S. and the European Union to act unilaterally. There is no consensus, however, on what the objectives of a labour clause in a multilateral trade agreement would look like. It is, however, instructive to think of a labour clause as a clause which aims to improve labour conditions in the Parties to a trade agreement. Such a clause may or may not allow trade sanctions to be taken.

The North American Agreement on Labour Cooperation offers one possible approach to negotiating a labour clause, and it may be a reasonable basis for engaging in a multilateral dialogue. The key feature of the NAALC approach is that there is no requirement to meet an internationally agreed standard. A multilateral application of the NAALC approach would allow each country to enforce its own domestic labour rights and standards as the "lowest" standard. This would act as a moral "ratchet effect" that would discourage countries from lowering their standards, but allow them to move to higher standards in accordance with their economic development. Moreover, lowering a domestic standard that was recognized in a multilateral agreement would likely have an electoral cost for a government.

A more ambitious multilateral approach would be to negotiate minimum labour rights and standards that would apply in all countries. This is distinct from the harmonization of labour rights and standards, which would be an even more ambitious undertaking. With the negotiation of minimum rights and standards, countries would be free to move unilaterally to a higher level. "High" minimum standards, such as on the notification period for layoffs or worker representation on firms' boards, might, however, generate rigidities in countries' economies. Diverse levels of economic development amongst countries also implies that minimum standards would have different effects in the countries concerned. This said, for some labour issues, such as health and safety and child and forced labour, there may be some scope for negotiating minimal standards. For a starting point in a minimum level negotiation, countries might turn to the work done by the International Labour Organization.

Since its establishment in 1919, the International Labour Organization has adopted more than 170 Conventions dealing with an extremely broad range of labour rights. The Conventions are only binding for countries that have ratified them. The ILO can also ask countries that have not ratified certain Conventions to report on their legislation and practice within the area covered by the Convention. The ILO may also investigate allegations that a country is denying workers' rights with regard to a Convention it has ratified, but has no enforcement powers to correct the country's actions. Moreover, there is no formal dispute settlement mechanism. In sum, pressure to abide by the Conventions is derived from moral suasion.[65] Concerns have also been expressed that the ILO, while well situated to play an institutional role in the labour-globalization interface, has failed to realize its potential in addressing labour issues. These concerns, however, may be diminishing as the ILO evolves into a more dynamic organization.[66]

The negotiation of a broad list of enforceable minimum labour rights and standards applying to all countries (whether or not in the context of a trade agreement) is probably not feasible at this time. The parties to the NAFTA did not negotiate minimum levels, and there is no indication that the political will exists for such a multilateral negotiation, one that would involve significantly more countries. A separate question is the scope of labour issues a multilateral negotiation would address. As mentioned earlier, the scope of the NAALC is fairly broad. The question of which labour standards should be included in a multilateral negotiation immediately arises. Van Liemt[67] has reviewed eight different proposals and found that a core group of standards were mentioned by all, and another three in at least six of the eight proposals reviewed:

- Freedom of association (ILO Convention 87).
- The right to organize and bargain collectively (Convention 98).

- Minimum age for the employment of children (Conventions 5 and 138).

- Freedom from discrimination in employment and occupation on the grounds of race, sex, religion, political opinion, etc. (Convention 111).
- Freedom from forced labour (Conventions 29 and 105).
- Occupational safety and health (various Conventions).

Canada has not ratified all of the labour conventions set out above. The Annex presents the ILO Conventions ratified by Canada. From the core group of standards identified by Van Liemt, Canada has not ratified the right to organize and bargain collectively (Convention 98) and the minimum age for the employment of children (Conventions 5 and 138). The U.S. has not ratified any of the Conventions within this core group. Of the remaining conventions set out above, with the exception of occupational safety and health conventions, the U.S. has only ratified the abolition of forced labour—Convention 105.[68]

The developing countries regard the developed countries as the "demandeurs" on the trade-labour issue. With the prospect of unilateral trade actions, the LDCs may eventually find it in their own interest to enter into multilateral negotiations. The developing countries may wish to seek concessions on labour mobility—the access to developed country markets for low skilled workers from the developing countries. Given the general concerns of the developing countries, particularly of a labour clause potentially adversely affecting or depriving them of one of their key comparative advantages, there is unlikely to be wide support for a broad negotiation on a global set of minimal labour standards. For multilateral negotiations, the developing countries may be more willing to accept a NAALC approach, one emphasising the importance of enforcing each country's own labour standards in at least some of the six labour areas set out above. Such an approach would allow for the accommodation of significant differences in the level of development of the participating countries.

The Domestic Arena: Domestic Labour Adjustment

The globalization process is likely to continue for the foreseeable future. There are no indications that firms wish to or can constrain their strategic business options and contain their varied activities within national boundaries. Globalization and free trade arrangements will challenge existing labour patterns. But it is difficult to identify the degree to which "global" as opposed to "domestic" factors influence the need for labour adjustment. The fundamental implication of globalization for labour markets is that national labour markets must be flexible and government and business policies and practices that develop human capital are to be encouraged. If the labour force is able to move quickly between different firms and industries, adjustment to sectoral shocks, from either "global" or "domestic" factors, would tend to create relatively less amounts of unemployment. However, if the labour force adjusts slowly, and labour released from declining sectors do not have the skills demanded by expanding sectors, there will be a relative increase in unemployment levels.

Globalization points to the need for domestic labour policy to become increasingly internationally market-oriented, rather than nationally focused. Due to the mobility of capital and technology, all countries need to establish labour policies which promote labour mobility and skill acquisition. To the extent that globalization encourages and increases the rate of technological transfer and the development of new technology, additional pressure will be placed on labour and the need for effective adjustment programs. The degree to which globalization contributes to structural unemployment, where both unemployment and job vacancies may rise, as opposed to cyclical unemployment, also implies that a different policy mix will be required, particularly one that puts greater emphasis on human skills development.

The emphasis on skills acquisition raises a question on the degree of emphasis on traditional policy objectives. Governments' labour and employment policies have traditionally been designed to achieve both equity and efficiency goals. Income support policies may be considered equity programs. These programs are designed to reduce the individual burden of workers who face job loss or some other form of dislocation from the work force. In contrast, job finding assistance and retraining or relocation assistance also have efficiency goals.

In keeping with this view of policy goals, the OECD has broken public expenditure on labour market policies into "active" and "passive" policy groups.[69] The "active" group of measures are considered as having the potential to achieve efficiency and equity objectives simultaneously, and includes expenditures on such measures as job search assistance, training and employment subsidies. "Passive" expenditures refer to income maintenance measures. OECD data (Chart 2) for 1985 (the first year for which data is available) and 1990 indicate that Canadian expenditure on "active" measures as a percentage of total labour market expenditures was lower than in most other OECD countries, and at least slightly less than that of the other G-7 countries. In Canada, the unemployment insurance program has come under criticism for being unable to deal effectively with unemployment and encouraging both workers and employers to avoid retraining or restructuring.[70] In particular, unemployment insurance has been criticized for adversely affecting the adjustment mechanism of the labour market by: contributing to an increase in the length of unemployment; contributing to an increase in the length of temporary layoffs; and by reinforcing the concentration of temporary and unstable jobs in high unemployment and low-wage regions.[71]

If Canadians are to continue to receive relatively high levels of total compensation, they will need to maintain relatively high levels of productivity growth. The external pressures mentioned earlier in the Paper mean that a globalized economy will not allow countries to maintain high wage-low skill production without some form of (economically inefficient) protection for the domestic economy. Canadian low-wage industries will face the greatest competitive challenge.

Chart 2
Expenditures on Active Programmes as a Percentage of Total Labour Market Expenditures

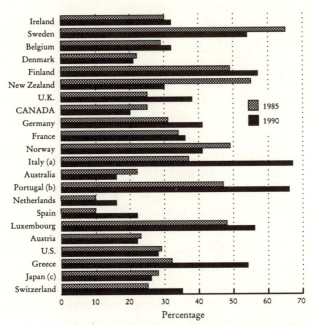

a) 1988 instead of 1990   b) 1986 instead of 1985   c) 1987 instead of 1985

Rugman and D'Cruz have concluded that the forces driving low-wage imports constitute a process that will continue until Canada's low-wage industries are forced out of business unless market niches are found.[72] The only other option would be for governments to provide some form of assistance or subsidization to protect industries, very much a second-best approach even over the short-term, as it would act as a productivity anchor on the economy as a whole.

SOME CONCLUSIONS AND OBSERVATIONS

THE GROWING INTERDEPENDENCE AND INTEGRATION of the world's economies require governments to give greater recognition to the global economy's implications for labour policies. Globalization and trade liberalization do not imply governments should take a laissez-faire approach. Rather, strategic refocussing is called for. With increased competition and restrictions on the use of traditional instruments to ease adjustment, governments have an increasingly important role in promoting human skill development.

The major conclusions and observations to be drawn from this Paper are:

- In respect of labour rights and standards, "social dumping" and "social countervail" should be approached very cautiously. Given the relative lack of unambiguous evidence on the effects of labour rights on wage costs, productivity differentials, and the risk of expanding the definition of a subsidy to include almost any differences in economic or social policies, Canada should oppose the introduction of such trade remedy mechanisms.
- If no workable multilateral understanding on trade-labour linkages is reached, however, there is a risk that unilateral trade measures will be used. In particular, it appears that the political climate in the U.S. is such that the U.S. could be prone to use unilateral measures if a multilateral mechanism is not available. As with its traditional approach to subsidization and other "unfair" trade practices, the U.S. is likely to be much more concerned with the "level" of its trading partners' labour laws and practices, rather than its own, such as "right to work" legislation in over 20 U.S. States.
- Canada should support further work internationally on labour rights and standards and their link to trade, primarily for three reasons: Canadian values favour the promotion of at least certain labour rights, including the prohibition of child or forced labour and the implementation of high work place safety standards; the failure to enforce labour rights and standards can have an impact on production costs—although the extent of the impact is not at all clear; and the blocking of work internationally that could lead to at least limited negotiations will only encourage the U.S. and the European Union to act unilaterally.
- Multilateral negotiations of trade-labour rights and standards along the lines of the North American Agreement

on Labour Cooperation, i.e., the enforcement of domestic laws, is the most practical approach to the issue. Agreement on a set of minimal rights and standards, or their harmonization, would be more challenging to negotiate. The best prospects for setting minimal labour rights may be in the areas of health and safety regulations, and the use of child or forced labour. The establishment of an effective and timely dispute settlement mechanism in such an agreement should be mandatory.
- Trade measures are not the only sanctions that a country could use in response to another country's "low," or failure to enforce, labour rights or standards. Another option is conditioning aid on the basis of a country's performance in the labour rights area. This could be coupled with a fines-based system as introduced in the North American Agreement on Labour Cooperation.
- There is a clear need for more empirical research on the issue, which only an international institution has the resources and multi-country contacts to undertake. A likely candidate to conduct such work would be a joint OECD committee bringing together the Directorate for Social Affairs, Manpower and Education, and the Trade Directorate. In January 1994, the U.S. began to explore and promote this option. It would be in the Canadian interest to support OECD analytical work on the issue.
- In the longer term, once the OECD has made progress on the analytical work, consideration should be given to the establishment of a GATT Working Group or a joint ILO/GATT Secretariat study group, in order to have broad developing country participation in the trade-labour dialogue. This suggestion is consistent with the International Trade Advisory Committee (ITAC) Task Force VIII (on Labour Practices and International Trade) recommendation that Canada support the proposal for the establishment of a GATT Working Party to examine the relationship between labour standards and international trade. A GATT Working Group on Labour could have a function similar to the former GATT Working Group on Environmental

Measures and International Trade; that is, to explore objectively the issue without passing judgement on the GATT consistency of countries' policies.
- It is questionable to what degree bringing labour rights into a multilateral agreement like the GATT will protect domestic Canadian firms from foreign competition.
- Effective labour adjustment policies in the developed countries which promote skills acquisition and labour mobility would likely reduce the public's and labour's concerns with trade liberalization and globalization.
- In the longer term, a failure to develop a flexible/high-skill work force could lead to more polarized income distribution and a reaction against market forces.
- Within Canada, because of the Constitutional division of legislative authority, there is a need for intergovernmental dialogue and cooperation. To facilitate Canada's possible participation in a multilateral dialogue, a joint federal-provincial task force to examine labour policies to address the adjustment pressures of globalization and global competition may be warranted. It is not too soon for trade and labour policymakers to start developing the appropriate expertise, implementing mechanisms for policy integration and planning for the challenge of a future multilateral negotiation which encompasses labour issues.
- Other stakeholders, business and labour organizations, need to participate in the domestic policy process. The globalization and labour issue promises to be an increasingly important element of the trade and investment policy agenda.[73]
- Canada is unlikely to have a competitive advantage in low-skilled industries. Consequently, domestic firms reliant upon low-skilled labour will face strong competition, and global firms reliant on low-skilled labour are unlikely to locate in Canada.
- Canada has taken steps to improve the system of training and adjustment programs available for Canadian labour. The pressure of globalization and trade liberalization are such that this type of strategy needs to continue. However,

adjustment pressures due to foreign competition as a result of globalization and trade liberalization should not be seen as fundamentally different from adjustment pressures arising from other reasons, such as shifts in consumer tastes, technological change or firms going out of business or reducing their labour force for any other reason.
- Demographic considerations must also be taken into account.[74] During the 1960s, 1970s and tapering off in the 1980s, the baby boom generation entered the work force, and labour force participation rates, particularly for women, increased. The Canadian labour market in the 1990s will face challenges arising from slower labour force growth and the aging of the labour force. Re-education and retraining of older workers will become increasingly important, as firms have been traditionally hesitant to retrain older workers.
- Globalization implies that, in addition to reviewing the equity and efficiency criteria of its domestic labour policies, Canada will need to review its immigration and refugee policies. To the extent that new immigrants are low-skilled labour, they may have greater difficulty than in the past finding employment in Canada. New low-skilled entrants to the labour market will also increase competition for the existing low-skill jobs in Canada.

FOOTNOTES

1. Wolfgang Michalski, "Support Policies for Strategic Industries: An Introduction to the Main Issues," in OECD, *Strategic Industries in a Global Economy: Policy Issues For The 1990's,* Paris 1991, p.13.
2. A. Weston, Ada Piazze-McMahon and Ed Dosman, "Free Trade with a Human Face? The Social Dimensions of CUSFTA and the Proposed NAFTA," The North-South Institute, Ottawa 1992, p.16.
3. Canadian Labour Market and Productivity Centre. *Canada: Meeting the Challenge of Change,* A Statement by the Economic Restructuring Committee of the CLMPC, Ottawa:CLMPC 1993, p.1.
4. The information and analysis presented in the next two sections may be familiar to a number of readers; hence these readers may wish to proceed directly to the section entitled "Canada: A Small, Open, Trade Dependent Economy."

5. Theodore Levitt, "The Globalization of Markets," *Harvard Business Review*, May-June 1983.
6. OECD, "Globalization Framework," TD/TC/WP(92)72, October 1992.
7. GATT, *International Trade 91-92*, Vol.II, p.1.
8. Keith Christie, *Globalization and Public Policy in Canada: In Search of a Paradigm*, DFAIT, Policy Staff Paper 93/01, January 1993, p.10.
9. IMF, *Direction of Trade Yearbook*.
10. GATT, *International Trade 91-92*, Vol.II, p.6.
11. Christie, *Globalization and Public Policy*, pp. 22-5.
12. John Rutter, "Recent Trends in International Direct Investment: The Boom Years Fade," U.S. Department of Commerce, August 1993.
13. *Ibid.*, Appendix Table 6.
14. Graham Vickery, "Global Industries and National Policies," in the *OECD Observer* 179, December 1992/January 1993.
15. Gary Clyde Hufbauer and Jeffrey Schott, *NAFTA An Assessment*, Institute for International Economics, 1993, p.19.
16. OECD, "Trade and Employment," C(89)42, 1989.
17. OECD, "Trade and Employment," C(89)42, Annex Summary Report, 1989, p.4.
18. OECD, "Symposium on Globalization of Industry: Government and Corporate Issues," DSTI/IND(93)29/Rev2, November 1993.
19. OECD, "Trade and Employment," C(89)42, 1989, p. 29.
20. OECD, "Trade and Employment," C(89)42, Annex Summary Report, p.1.
21. Statistics Canada, Preliminary Statement of Canadian International Trade October 1993, Statistics Canada: 65-001 p. Vol. 9, No. 10, December 1993.
22. IMF, *Financial Statistics Yearbook*.
23. Gordon Betcherman, "Labour in a More Global Economy," a paper prepared for the Office of International Affairs, Human Resources and Labour Canada, 1993.
24. Direct investment (assets and liabilities), as defined by Statistics Canada, represents the investment which allows an investor to influence or to have a voice in the management of an enterprise. For operational purposes, a direct investor usually has the ownership of at least 10 per cent of the equity in an enterprise; all long-term claims of the enterprise with the direct investor are classified as direct investment. Direct investment reflect the values measured from the books of the issuing companies. Statistics Canada, *Canada's International Investment Position*, Statistics Canada: 67-202,1993, p.41.
25. Dennis Seebach, *Globalization: The Impact on the Trade and Investment Dynamic*, DFAIT, Policy Staff Paper 93/07, June 1993, p.37.
26. *Ibid.*, p. 41.

27. Government of Canada, *Employment Standards Legislation in Canada,* Minister of Supply and Services Canada, 1991.
28. Labour Canada, "Comparison of Labour Legislation of General Application In Canada, the United States and Mexico," 1991.
29. The Agreement came into effect on the same day as the NAFTA, 1 January 1994.
30. Preamble to the North American Free Trade Agreement.
31. This section is based on the Economic Council of Canada, *Adjustment Policies for Trade-Sensitive Industries,* Economic Council of Canada, 1988.
32. Canadian Labour Congress,"Submission by the Canadian Labour Congress on the North American Free Trade Agreement to the Sub-Committee on International Trade of the Standing Committee on External Affairs and International Trade," 26 January 1993.
33. Jim Stanford, *Going South. Cheap Labour as an Unfair Subsidy in North American Free Trade,* Canadian Centre for Policy Alternatives, Ottawa, December 1991, p.18.
34. A. Weston, et al., "Free Trade with a Human Face?," p.17.
35. *The Globe and Mail* ("Mexico Wage Debate," 5 November 1993, p.B1). Only toward the end of the article, in two short sentences, is it noted that Mexican labour's productivity is lower than its U.S. counterpart. Similarly, *The Ottawa Citizen,* 7 November 1993, p.C4, makes wage comparisons between autoworkers in Canada, the U.S. and Mexico, but fails to mention differences in productivity.
36. U.S. Department of Labor, Bureau of Labor Statistics, "International Comparisons of Hourly Compensation Costs for Production Workers in Manufacturing," Report 844, April 1993, p.13.
37. Business International Corporation, *Investing Licensing And Trading Conditions Abroad. Americas,* September 1992.
38. U.S. Department of Labor, Bureau of Labor Statistics, "International Comparisons of Hourly Compensation Costs for Production Workers in Manufacturing," Report 844, April 1993. The Bureau of Labor Statistics' compensation measures are computed in national currency units and are converted into U.S. dollars at prevailing market exchange rates. The measures do not indicate the relative living standards nor the purchasing power of income. Moreover, total compensation measures, even on a purchasing power basis, are poor indicators of relative living standards, as taxation rates vary, both direct and indirect, and thus even if pre-taxation compensation levels were the same, disposable income (what really counts for workers) would vary.
39. Department of Finance, Canada, "The North American Free Trade Agreement: An Economic Assessment From A Canadian Perspective," November 1992, p.51. The analysis by the Department of Finance is based on 1989 data.

40. See Ann Weston, "Social Subsidies and Trade with Developing Countries," a paper prepared for the Ontario Government, North-South Institute, 1991, for an illustrative list of various definitions of "social dumping" or "social subsidies".
41. International Labor Rights Education and Research Fund, *Trade's Hidden Costs,* 1988. Page 25 cites some examples where service sector jobs in the U.S. were allegedly transferred to foreign countries. The National Association of Working Women believed that "substandard" practices abroad could result in firms using the threat of moving jobs overseas to block organizing efforts by clerical workers in the U.S..
42. GATT, Basic Instruments and Selected Documents (BISD) Volume IV, Text of the General Agreement, 1969, Geneva:GATT,1986.
43. Jim Stanford, *Going South.*
44. Morley Gunderson and Anil Verma, "Canadian Labour Policies and Global Competition," *The Canadian Business Law Journal,* Volume 20, 1992.
45. J.M. Servais, "The Social Clause in Trade Agreements: Wishful Thinking or an Instrument of Social Progress?," *International Labour Review,* Vol. 129, No. 6, p.427.
46. Gus Edgren, "Fair Labour Standards and Trade Liberalisation," *International Labour Review,* Vol. 118, No.5, Sep-Oct 1979, p. 529.
47. Gary S. Fields, "Labour Standards, Economic Development, and International Trade," in S. Herzenberg and J. Perez-Lopez, *Labour Standards and Development in the Global Economy,* US Department of Labour, 1990.
48. *Ibid.*, p.27.
49. A firm's competitive situation, which would be affected by higher wages, would, of course, also depend upon the firm's productivity, as discussed earlier in this Paper. The point here is that wages may rise in the absence of "strong" labour rights.
50. Section 6306(b) of the U.S.'s Omnibus Trade and Competitiveness Act of 1988 requires the Secretary of Labour to prepare a biennial report to Congress, identifying the extent to which countries recognize and enforce internationally recognized worker rights. These rights include: freedom of association, the right to form unions and bargain collectively, abolition of forced labour, limits on child labour and minimum standards for working conditions.
51. Labour Canada, "Comparison of Labour Legislation of General Application In Canada, the United States and Mexico," March 1991.
52. S. Hecker and M. Hallock, "Introduction: Labour in a Global Economy," in S. Hecker and M. Hallock, eds., *Labour in a Global Economy: Perspectives from the US and Canada.* Eugene, Oregon, University of Oregon, 1991, p.5.

53. GATT, L/6243, 28 October 1987.
54. J.F. Perez-Lopez, "Conditioning Trade on Foreign Labour Law: The U.S. Approach," *Comparative Labour Law Journal*, Vol.9, Number 2, 1988, p.256.
55. *Ibid.*, p. 257.
56. *Ibid.*
57. *Ibid.*, p. 280.
58. GATT, L/6243, 28 October 1987.
59. GATT, L/6729, 21 September 1990.
60. Gijsbert van Liemt, "Minimum Labour Standards and International Trade: Would a Social Clause Work?," in *International Labour Review*, Vol. 128, No. 4, 1989.
61. Cited in van Liemt. Section 502(b)(8) of the 1984 Trade and Tariff Act.
62. *Ibid.*
63. Public Law 100-418, 100th USA Congress.
64. Editor's Note: The 1994 election of Republican majorities in both Houses of Congress will complicate the domestic management of this matter in the U.S.. But the trade and labour issue is unlikely to fade away entirely, much less permanently.
65. Gus Edgren, "Fair Labour Standards and Trade Liberalisation," *International Labour Review*, Vol. 118, No.5, Sept-Oct 1979, p. 527.
66. As with a number of other international organizations, the ILO has been criticized in some quarters for failing to realize its potential. The ILO is tripartite in nature (government, business and the labour movement). Canadian business has perceived the organization as being dominated by labour interests and has not actively participated in the ILO's activities. The ILO has also been seen as being dominated by European interests, with the ILO's bureaucracy resistant to reform. Discussions with Canadian government officials indicate that Canadian business is now taking a more positive interest in the organization, and that the ILO is evolving into a more dynamic organization with a greater ability to address the labour-globalization interface. See Gordon Betcherman, "Labour in a More Global Economy," a paper prepared for the Office of International Affairs, Human Resources and Labour Canada, 1993, pp. 19-20.
67. Van Liemt, "Minimum Labour Standards," p. 437.
68. Of the parties to the NAFTA, the U.S. had ratified 9 ILO Conventions, Mexico 66 and Canada 27, as of December 1993.
69. OECD, *Progress In Structural Reform: An Overview*, 1992.
70. A. Weston, et al., "Free Trade with a Human Face?," p.28.
71. M. J. Trebilcock, M. Chandler and R. Howse, with the collaboration of P. Simm, *Adjusting to Trade: A Comparative Perspective*, Economic Council of Canada Discussion Paper No.358, October 1988. Also see J. Cousineau, "Unemployment Insurance and

Labour Market Adjustments," *Income Distribution and Economic Security in Canada,* Vol. 1, Research Studies for Royal Commission on Economic Union and Development Prospects, 1985.
72. Alan M.Rugman and Joseph D'Cruz, "Canadian Strategies for International Competitiveness," *Business in the Contemporary World,* Volume III, Number 1, 1990, pp.96-8.
73. A widely held view is that Canadian employers provide less training to their workers than those in other OECD countries. A recent study by Constantine Kapsalis, "Employee Training in Canada: Reassessing the Evidence," *Canadian Business Economics,* Summer 1993, pp.3-11, challenges this view. Kapsalis concluded that there is no evidence that Canadian employers train less than employers in other industrial countries, but that there is also "wide scope for much greater synergy among educational institutions, business, labour, and government in providing training. The training gap that needs to be filled in Canada is not in the resources devoted to training, but in the development of more innovative ways of building on the strengths of all labour market partners and helping individuals with labour market difficulties to integrate successfully into the labour market."
74. See David K. Foot and Kevin J. Gibson, "Population Aging in the Canadian Labour Force: Changes and Challenges," *Journal of Canadian Studies,* Vol.28, No. 1, Spring 1993.

ANNEX

ILO Conventions Ratified by Canada

1. Hours of Work (Industry) Convention, 1919
(Ratified by Canada March 21, 1935)
7. Minimum Age (Sea) Convention, 1920
(Ratified March 31, 1926)
8. Unemployment Indemnity (Shipwreck) Convention, 1920
(Ratified March 31, 1926)
14. Weekly Rest (Industry) Convention, 1921
(Ratified March 21, 1935)
15. Minimum Age (Trimmers and Stokers) Convention, 1921
(Ratified March 31, 1926)
16. Medical Examination of Young Persons (Sea) Convention, 1921
(Ratified March 31,1926)
22. Seamen's Articles of Agreement Convention, 1926
(Ratified June 30, 1938)
26. Minimum Wage-Fixing Machinery Convention,1928
(Ratified April 25, 1935)
27. Marking of Weight (Packages Transported by Vessels) Convention, 1929
(Ratified June 30, 1938)
32. Protection Against Accidents (Dockers) Convention (Revised), 1932
(Ratified April 6, 1946)
58. Minimum Age (Sea) Convention (Revised), 1936
(Ratified September 10, 1951)
63. Convention Concerning Statistics of Wages and Hours of Work, 1938
(Ratified April 6, 1946)
68. Food and Catering (Ships' Crews) Convention, 1946
(Ratified by March 19, 1951)
69. Certification of Ships' Cooks Convention, 1946
(Ratified March 19, 1951)
73. Medical Examination (Seafarers) Convention, 1946
(Ratified March 19,1951)

74. Certification of Able Seamen Convention, 1946
(Ratified March 19, 1951)
80. Final Articles Revision Convention, 1946
(Ratified July 31, 1947)
87. Freedom of Association and Protection of the Right to Organise Convention, 1948
(Ratified March 23, 1972)
88. Employment Service Convention, 1948
(Ratified August 24, 1950)
100. Equal Remuneration Convention, 1951
(Ratified November 16, 1972)
105. Abolition of Forced Labour Convention, 1957
(Ratified July 14, 1959)
108. Seafarers' Identity Documents Convention, 1958
(Ratified May 31, 1967)
111. Discrimination (Employment and Occupation) Convention, 1958
(Ratified November 26, 1964)
116. Final Articles Revision Convention, 1961
(Ratified by April 5, 1962)
122. Employment Policy Convention, 1964
(Ratified September 16, 1966)
162. Asbestos Convention, 1986
(Ratified June 16, 1988)
147. Merchant Shipping (Minimum Standards) Convention, 1976
(Ratified June 1, 1993)

ANNEX

Policy Staff Papers/Documents du groupe des politiques

Recent Papers on Economic and Trade Policy Issues/ Récents documents sur des questions économiques et de politique commerciale:

A) Trade Policy Series

1. *Globalization and Public Policy in Canada: In Search of a Paradigm,* by Keith H. Christie. 93/01 (January 1993) * SP19
2. *Trade and the Environment: Dialogue of the Deaf or Scope for Cooperation?,* by Michael Hart and Sushma Gera. 92/11 (June 1992) SP18
3. *Globalization: The Impact on the Trade and Investment Dynamic,* by Dennis Seebach. 93/07 (June 1993) * SP25
4. *Merger Control Under Trade Liberalization: Convergence or Cooperation?* by Nicolas Dimic. 93/09 (August 1993) * SP27
5. *Technology Consortia: A Prisoner's Dilemma?* by Rhoda Caldwell. 93/10 (August 1993) * SP28
6. *Optimal Patent Term and Trade: Some Considerations on the Road Ahead* by I. Prakash Sharma. 93/12 (October 1993) * SP30
7. *And the Devil Take the Hindmost: The Emergence of Strategic Trade Policy* by I. Prakash Sharma and Keith H. Christie. 93/14 (December 1993) * SP32
8. *Stacking the Deck: Compliance and Dispute Settlement in International Environmental Agreements* by Keith H. Christie. 93/15 (December 1993) * SP33
9. *Financial Market Integration: The Effects on Trade and the Responses of Trade Policy,* by James McCormack. 94/01 (February 1994) * SP35
10. *The New Jerusalem: Globalization, Trade Liberalization, and Some Implications for Canadian Labour Policy,* by Rob Stranks. 94/02 (February 1994) * SP36

11. *Competition Policy Convergence: The Case of Export Cartels,* by William Ehrlich and I. Prakash Sharma. 94/03 (April 1994) SP37
12. *The Day After: An Agenda for Diversifying Free Trade,* by Keith H. Christie. 94/04 (January 1994) * SP38
13. *Global Strategies and Foreign Direct Investment: Implications for Trade and the Canadian Economy,* by Julie Fujimura. 94/07 (March 1994) * SP41
14. *Delivering the Goods: Manufacturer-Retailer Relations and The Implications for Competition and Trade Policies,* by I. Prakash Sharma and Prue Thomson, with Keith H. Christie. 94/11 (December 1994) SP45
15. *Le libre-échange nord-américain, les subventions et les droits compensateurs: la problématique et les options,* par Gilbert Gagné. 94/13 (Juillet 1994). SP47
16. *Dangerous Liaisons: The World Trade Organization and the Environmental Agenda,* by Anne McCaskill. 94/14 (June 1994) SP48
17. *Damned If We Don't: Some Reflections On Antidumping and Competition Policy,* by Keith H. Christie. 94/15 (July 1994) SP49
18. *Pandora's Box?: Countervailing Duties and the Environment,* by Robert T. Stranks. 94/19 (October 1994) SP53

B) Trade Development Series

1. *From a Trading Nation to a Nation of Traders: Towards a Second Century of Trade Development,* by Andrew Griffith. 92/05 (March 1992) SP12
2. *Exports and Job Creation,* by Morley Martin. 93/06 (June 1993) * SP24
3. *The Impact of Exports: An Input-Output Analysis of Canadian Trade,* by James McCormack. 94/24 (December 1994) SP58

C) *Regional Trade and Economic Series*

1. *Different Strokes: Regionalism and Canada's Economic Diplomacy,* by Keith H. Christie. 93/08 (May 1993) * SP26
2. *Japan Trading Corp.: Getting the Fundamentals Right* by I. Prakash Sharma. 93/16 (December 1993) * SP34
3. *Canada in the Americas: New Opportunities and Challenges,* by Conrad Sheck, Colin Robertson, Jamal Khokhar, Nicolas Dimic, and Keith Christie. 94/06 (April 1994) * SP40
4. *China 2000: The Nature of Growth and Canada's Economic Interests,* by Stephen Lavergne. 94/10 (May 1994) SP44
5. *The Japanese Way: The Relationship Between Financial Institutions and Non-Financial Firms,* by James McCormack. 94/16 (July 1994) SP50
6. *Towards Regional Economic Blocs: Are We There Yet?,* by Julie Fujimura. 95/01 (February 1995) SP 59
7. *Changing Partners: Trends in Canada's Regional Economic Relations,* by Steve Wilson. 95/02 (March 1995) SP60
8. *Fact or Fancy?: North Asia Economic Integration,* by Stephen Lavergne. 95/03 (March 1995) SP43

D) *Other Economic Papers*

1. *World Population Growth and Population Movements: Policy Implications for Canada,* by Michael Shenstone. 92/07 (April 1992) SP14
2. *Pour des sanctions efficaces et appropriées,* par Jean Prévost. 93/04 (mars 1993) * SP22
3. *Black Gold: Developments in the World Oil Market and the Implications for Canada,* by Sushma Gera. 93/05 (February 1993) * SP23
4. *Determinants of Economic Growth in Developing Countries: Evidence and Canadian Policy Implications,* by Rick Mueller. 94/08 (April 1994) * SP42

5. *Still an Albatross? The LDC Debt Crisis Revisited,* by Rick Mueller. 94/09 (May 1994) SP43
6. *Pro-Active Sanctions: A New/Old Approach to Non-Violent Measures,* by Dr. Nicholas Tracy. 94/17 (June 1994) SP51A
7. *A View of the Forest: Environmental Stress, Violent Conflict and National Security,* by Robert T. Stranks. 95/05 (April 1995) SP63

Policy Staff Commentaries*

1. The Uruguay Round: What's In It For The Developing Countries, by Robert T. Stranks. (March 1994)
2. Outward Direct Investment: Implications for Domestic Employment, by Robert T. Stranks and Julie Fujimura. (April 1994)
3. Trade and Direct Investment Statistics: The Twain Have Met, by James McCormack. (May 1994)
4. Economic Sanctions: Foreign Policy Foil or Folly?, by Robert T. Stranks. (May 1994)
5. Recent Capital Flows to Latin America: Too Good to Last?, by Richard E. Mueller. (August 1994)
6. Not Out of the (Bretton) Woods Yet: Exchange Rate Disequilibria, Trade and Suggested Reforms, by James McCormack. (February 1995)
7. Takin' Care of Business: The Impact of Deficit Reduction on the Trade Sector, by James McCormack. (March 1995)

* available in English/disponible en français